THE STRAIGHT DOWN LOW!
A REVEALING AND CONTROVERSIAL EXPOSÉ
ABOUT THE DECADE'S #1 R& B STAR

R. Kelly's distinct sound has an ability to blend "cutting edge, street-wise Hip-Hop music and storytelling with smooth love songs. His role as collaborative composer and producer with other artists expanded outside of his R&B genre, reflecting the diversity of his talents, as he crafted hits for many of the world's biggest Pop stars, including Michael Jackson, Celine Dion, Notorious BIG, Puffy, Janet Jackson, Toni Braxton, Mary J. Blige, NAS, Maxwell, Kirk Franklin, and KC & Jo Jo.

In *Your Body's Calling Me: Music, Love, Sex and Money—The Story of the Life and Times of "Robert" R. Kelly*, author Jake Brown explores the past of R. Kelly in the hopes of uncovering the truth behind his celebrated, yet conflicted life.

- ▼ His childhood and impoverished upbringir
- ▼ His abuse as a child.
- ▼ Experiences that molded him into both the
- ▼ His collaboration with and marriage to Aaliyah.
- ▼ Child porn allegations filed against him.
- ▼ His haunting past.
- ▼ The God-fearing, Soul, and Rhythm and Blues sounds that led him to a chart-topping career.

R. Kelly, musical genius, racked up numerous Top 40 and Top 10 smash hits in Billboard's Top 200 list. His music has topped Billboard's R&B Album, Adult Contemporary, Hot 100 Singles and Albums and the R&B/Hip Hop Charts. R. Kelly has been nominated for and received numerous awards including: Grammys for Best Male R&B Vocal Performance, Best R&B Album, and Best Rap Performance by a Duo or Group; Soul Train Music Awards for Best R&B/Soul Album, Male; NAACP Image Awards for Outstanding Male Artist and Music Video, and was the American Music Award's Favorite Male Soul/R&B Artist and Sammy Davis Jr. Entertainer of the Year.

In an instant, R. Kelly would go from a revered global superstar with a musical talent that he had once characterized as "the only thing I have to lean on" to a man whose very foundation of support was being threatened in terms of its applicable relevance in the fight to save him.

The embattled R&B star R. Kelly was arrested on a fugitive nationwide warrant issued as he was preparing to leave a rented vacation home where he had lived for more than a year with his wife and three children... charged with 21 counts of child pornography.

In an instant, R. Kelly would go from a revered global superstar to a man whose freedom, security, whose very foundation was being threatened.

Your Body's Calling Me reveals all the details about how R. Kelly became the "Prince of Pillowtalk" and how that title would come back to haunt him....again....and again...

Your Body's Calling Me Music, Love, Sex & Money

The Life & Times of "Robert" R. Kelly

By Jake Brown

Colossus Books

Phoenix
New York   Los Angeles

YOUR BODY'S CALLING ME
Music, Love, Sex & Money
The Life & Times of "Robert" R. Kelly
By Jake Brown

Published by:
Colossus Books
A Division of Amber Communications Group, Inc.
1334 East Chandler Boulevard, Suite 5-D67
Phoenix, Z 85048
amberbk@aol.com
WWW.AMBERBOOKS.COM

Tony Rose, Publisher/Editorial Director   Samuel P. Peabody, Associate Publisher
Yvonne Rose, Senior Editor   The Printed Page, Interior Design/Cover Layout
Edited by Yvonne Fleetwood
Cover Design by Yvonne Rose
Front and back cover photos: Reisig & Taylor
Inside photos: Raymond Boyd, Walik Goshorn

ISBN#: 0-9727519-5-5

Library of Congress Cataloging-In-Publication Data

Brown, Jake.
    Your body's calling me : music, love, sex & money : the life & times of "Robert" R. Kelly
/ by Jake Brown.
        p. cm.
    ISBN 0-9727519-5-5
    1. Kelly, R. 2. Rhythm and blues musicians--United States--Biography. I. Title.

ML420.K3B76 2003
782.421643'092--dc21
[B]
                                        2003053300

Contents

Prologue: Redemption

2004 has started out a lot better than 2003 did for R. Kelly, and certainly has continued to add distance to the latter half of 2002, which was arguably the darkest period in R. Kelly's otherwise star-bright career. In the legal arena, Kelly has been partially exonerated in his child pornography case after 7 of the 21 counts lodged against him were dismissed on in the Illinois case, which his defense team termed "the first official acknowledgement of the weakness of (the prosecution's) case."

Across the country in Florida, Kelly also scored a major legal victory on March 11, 2004, when, as MTV News reported, "a judge ruled…that digital photographs allegedly showing R. Kelly having sex with an underage girl were illegally obtained by Florida detectives and therefore cannot be used to try him on child-pornography charges in that state, *The Associated Press* reports…Kelly, 37, currently faces 12 counts of child pornography in Florida, where deputies seized a digital camera—wrapped in a towel in a duffel bag—during a June 2002 drug raid of his Davenport home.

If prosecutors do not appeal the March 11 ruling, they would have to drop all charges against Kelly in Florida." Meanwhile, in his professional life, Kelly has been flying as high as he believed he could in song, on the charts, on tour, in award nominations, and even on Broadway!

In the spirit of his fighting mood, R. Kelly started this year out in negotiations to score the Broadway musical based on the Sylvester

Stallone classic Rocky, which won Best Picture at the 1976 Academy Awards.

Even more at odds with the media portrayal of Kelly in the press over the year prior, the controversial singer was nominated on January 18th, 2004 for an IMAGE AWARD for Outstanding Album. In addition, he won the 2004 QUINCY JONES AWARD for "Outstanding Career Achievements, Male" and the 2004 SOUL TRAIN AWARD for "Best R&B/Soul Album, Male" for *Chocolate Factory.*

Kelly's legal team and record label had managed to harness the media hype surrounding the charges between 2002 and early 2003 into a lightening bolt that kept shocking fans as the months inevitably wore on—not with more tabloid stories, but rather with smash hits and critical accolades surrounding the release of Kelly's latest solo offering, 'The Chocolate Factory', which sold 532,000 copies in its Top 10 debut week, and which remained in the Billboard Top 40 for the entirety of 2003.

It was a brilliant public relations strategy, giving the public a light other than controversy in which to view Kelly, a familiar light that made him shine to fans like the star they had embraced for the past 14 years. Kelly hadn't reinvented himself, rather he'd reinvented the focus of the media coverage surrounding him—from speculation over the charges against him to matter-of-fact, across-the-board praise over his talent.

Kelly's lead single off of his latest album, 'Ignition', had been his biggest hit in years, arguably since 'I Believe I Can Fly'. A number one smash on both the Billboard Singles and R&B Charts, the song was also aptly titled for the intention R. Kelly had with it, to jumpstart his career where the legal charges against him had stalled it a year earlier. Not only did 'Ignition' get luck going for Kelly in a different direction than it had been heading, the song also reminded the prosecutors of exactly what they were up against with their pursuit of the performer.

Not only was he winning the public (i.e. his potential jury pool) back over, Kelly was being aided in his quest by the presiding Judge in the case, who had granted him a wide array of legal latitude in the course of rehabilitating his public image. In addition to allowing Kelly to leave the State of Illinois for video shoots to support the release of his album and radio singles (i.e. his image rehabilitation), his honor also allowed Kelly to tour before hundreds of thousands of his fans, and even to attend nationally televised Award shows like the Grammies and Billboard Music Awards. Though the Judge was required by law to allow Kelly a certain amount of latitude in earning a living, prosecutors fought Kelly's every trip along the way.

The gamble in this strategy was not only in the chance that the Judge would rule in Kelly's favor, but that it would reflect in the watching public's conscience toward an impression that the gravity of the charges against him were less serious than they might seem given two things: A.) that R. Kelly was doing a successful job of battling the allegations against him in the public image arena, and B.) that the presiding judge who could very well sentence Kelly to multiple years in jail upon conviction was helping the performer in his attempts to better himself to potential jurors.

Likely in the judge's eyes, he was just doing his job, affording the defendant his Constitutionally-guaranteed right to the presumption of innocence, but the reality of Kelly's drive to prove himself as something other than the monster prosecutors hoped he would be seen as to the American public was resonating with everyone.

The media, after a while, seemed to come around to this notion, exemplified in a USA TODAY editorial on Kelly's case in early 2003, "Of course, no matter how suggestive his lyrics, Kelly is entitled to the presumption of innocence...Kelly needs to go on the offensive. Like it or not, high-profile cases such as this one are often judged in the court of public opinion long before a jury gets to render a decision." The performer's successes over the course of

2003 reflects a well-oiled machine working behind the scenes to make sure Kelly had every opportunity to succeed—his record label pumping millions of dollars into the promotion of his new album, his legal team working around the clock to battle the charges against him on any merit the law might afford, his fans doing their part by embracing Kelly's new product and image as consumers.

Kelly was operating on a tightrope where the balance was ironically maintained by the fact that he had everything to lose, and everything to gain, all at the same time. A review of Kelly's highlights from 2003 give the impression that he was riding high, at the top of his game, and in fact he was, in spite of the legal charges and their potential implications hanging over him. What motivated Kelly most seemed to be the fact that he stood to lose not only his freedom, but everything professionally that he had worked for, leading up to the point where he faced the reality of losing both. Perhaps one was worthless to him without the other?

In either case, Kelly was motivated, and the industry seemed intent on rallying around his cause. Not only did his peers largely suspend any vocal speculation in the press about his potential guilt, one way or the other, despite the existing reputation Kelly had on that subject, they also sought him out in collaboration after collaboration.

This latter point is remarkably important because of the reality that each artist who associated professionally with Kelly risked potential damage to their own career if their fan bases didn't approve. That they chose to proceed in spite of this possibility illustrated the extent of their confidence in either Kelly's innocence, or his ability to overcome the adversity of his legal troubles with good, old fashioned talent. As Suge Knight once wisely proclaimed in an interview with the Source, "As long as there's money rolling in, (the industry) will deal with you."

Perhaps that fact also played a role in Kelly's collaborations over the course of 2003, but he sure seemed to have a lot of peers in his corner. Not only lining up to work with Kelly, many of the biggest names in the business have gone on record in their support of Kelly, including rap's most potent star of the millennium thus far, 50 Cent, who told MTV that "He's still the best in R&B...even with the trouble...The other artists that's coming out, half of them it's his song he wrote for them. It's obvious that he's the better, the stronger (artist)." Rapper Ludacris agreed, explaining that it's simply impossible not to love R. Kelly for his talent, "R. Kelly is definitely the king of R&B...I'm a fan. Even if you don't like him, you can't not like his music. There's no way. You can try to not like his music, but it's gonna get your ass eventually, for sure."

Heavy set rapper Fat Joe gave a more impassioned endorsement of Kelly, pointing out that fans can't differentiate between R. Kelly the performer and R. Kelly the potential criminal once they choose his music over the speculative hype, proclaiming that "He's the best... If you love music, you love R. Kelly. I just heard the remix to 'Ignition,' it's phenomenal...'Can I get a toot toot! Can I get a beep beep!' I was like, 'Oooohhhhh! Oh my God! What is this?' That's that thing, man. The R. gives you that, man!" Bad Boy Records and Sean Jean Clothing C.E.O. Sean 'P. Diddy' Combs was analyical on the matter of Kelly's resilient popularity, both within the industry and among music listeners, explaining that for him, and likely for millions of others, its a matter of giving Kelly the benefit of the doubt until the facts prove otherwise, even in light of the graphic nature of the evidence against him, "When I saw the joint, I was like, 'Whoa,'...I mean, the first couple of (scenes), my man was a straight porno star. Then as it got towards the end (of the tape) it was like, 'Whoa, whoa, whoa.' But you don't know unless you were there...We have to wait till the truth comes out, and I just pray for him that he has a brighter day coming. I ain't going to abandon him (in the meanwhile)."

That seemed to be the general sentiment throughout the industry, with prominent examples included the Isley Brothers' *Body Kiss*, a number one album Kelly almost entirely wrote and produced, as well as hits for B2K ("Bump, Bump, Bump," "Girlfriend," "What a Girl Wants"), Ginuwine ("Hell Yeah"), Marques Houston ("Clubbin' ") and Nick Cannon ("Gigolo"), as well as songs Kelly wrote during this time for upcoming albums by Britney Spears, Michael Jackson, Missy Elliott, Jennifer Lopez, Ruben Studdard, the Big Tymers and Tyrese, as well as a full length follow-up to 2002's Jay Z collaboration LP 'Best of Both Worlds', this time around with Baby of the Cash Money Records clique, entitled 'Best of Both Worlds 2'.

Not bad for 12 months. In the award show category, Kelly faired equally as well, taking home four Billboard Awards (Hot 100 Producer, R&B Producer, Hot 100 Songwriter and R&B Songwriter) where he also performed live with 'Step in the Name of Love', attending the BMI Urban Awards in Miami in August, and racking up 2 Grammy Nominations, but it was in the live arena where Kelly made his biggest splash over the course of 2003. Over loud protests from Prosecutors, Kelly was permitted by Judge Vincent Gaughan to embark on two separate legs of his 'Chocolate Factory' tour, speaking directly to hundreds of thousands of his fans and padding his bank account with millions of dollars likely to go directly to his legal team's round-the-clock battle to exonerate the superstar.

Kelly's first leg began in the summer, taking him to the Oakland-Alameda County Arena in Oakland, California, on August 15; the Great Western Forum in Inglewood, California, on August 16; the MCI Center in Washington, D.C., on August 22; Madison Square Garden in New York on August 23; and the Philips Arena in Atlanta on August 28, while the second leg commenced in October across the South and East Coast, hitting Houston's Toyota Center on October 25; the New Orleans Arena on October 26; Philadelphia's Wachovia Center on October 31; and Hampton, Virginia's Hampton Coliseum on November 1.

Seeming kinetically in touch with his audience, Kelly, on one date at New York City's Madison Square Garden, told his sold-out crowd that "my fans have given me so many hits…I love y'all. I don't know what to perform next. Y'all gotta tell me what song to sing." At another point in the show, the reality of Kelly's pending legal situation seemed to weigh in on him even as he gave the sold-out arena his all in spite of it, remarking at one point that "Even under the circumstances, I gotta do what I do. Is that all right?"

Kelly was in the zone throughout the year, performing extraordinarily well under the pressure, shoring up his fan support by giving them hits, as well as industry support by making everyone who worked with him a ton of money. Above all else, R. Kelly proved over the course of 2003 that he still had it, and that professionally, he was in better shape than ever, and well worth taking a risk on, in that sense.

Following up the success of 'Chocolate Factory', Kelly dished fans a second disc inside of the same year, this time '*The R. in R&B Collection Vol. 1*', released in October of 2003. Featuring yet another new single 'Thoia Thoing', which of course became an immediate chart topping hit, the song propelled the 23-track hits collection to a #4 debut on Billboard's Top 200 Albums Chart, logging over 250,000 copies in its first week.

Much to the dread of prosecutors, Kelly also announced that he had 2 new albums worth of material scheduled for release in 2004, including his collaboration with Baby from the Cash Money Clique, who spoke glowingly of the album in the late fall of 2003 as its recording wound down, "Me and Kelly are almost finished…It's kind of a combination with both (singing and rapping). Dude is doing his thing, I'm doing my thing with it. We worked together on every song, so me and his ideas came together so big it's just gonna be one of them kind of albums."

The duo got along so handsomely that they also co-wrote a screenplay for a movie, 'Eye Contact', which they began shooting on location in Miami and Chicago in late 2003. By putting himself back on top of the charts, Kelly lifted himself above the controversy surrounding his legal situation. He gave his critics and fans alike something else to talk about, his remarkable musical talent, and indomitable ability to raise everyone's spirits, including is own.

Both the songs from 'Chocolate Factory', released after he had been formally arraigned and charged on charges, and the new material off Kelly's Greatest Hits collection, were bold and proud, unapologetically sexual, i.e. exactly what Kelly's fans needed from the performer, and reciprocally what he needed from them in terms of their embrace, "Y'all showed me so much love…[The success,] it's because of my fans. Y'all supported me through the storm, and I'mma keep on giving it as long as you want it."

America is a forgiving public— especially for societally relevant or beloved celebrities, those who aren't 15 minute famers, but whose fame is a by-product of their positive contribution to real people's everyday lives. This is especially true with musicians, actors, politicians—the types of public figures whose actions change people's lives on a mainstream level for the better.

That aside, people are curious in general about the private lives of celebrities, and tend to tolerate a wide array of indiscretions on the part of their favorite stars because the public wants to forgive a celebrity for something they—the reader—would personally never get away with in their own life. Kelly has benefited from this latitude in the course of his career, a prominent example being the silence in public reaction one way or the other, over his illegal marriage to 15-year-old Aaliyah in 1995.

Still, this public fascination is also a point Kelly lamented in an interview in 2003 with *Blender Magazine* after the downside of public curiosity over a celebrity in the 'art imitating life vs. life imitating art' curiosity caught up with him in the context of his legal troubles, "It's hard being me. But it's always been hard being me. It's hard to be famous and free. Everybody wants to know: 'What are you going to write?' People assume that what I say in a song shows what kind of person I am...how good or bad I am."

The American public forgave Bill Clinton's personal indiscretions because his political management of the economy was so positive for the country in general. Because the allegations against R. Kelly are personal in nature, he has been given a professional reprieve until such time as his trial exonerates him in the way his fans already have.

A *Chicago Tribune* article echoed the latter, quoting B-96 Program Director Todd Cavanah, pointed out that "Kelly is not the first celebrity in recent years to weather a sex scandal. 'People like President Clinton paved the way...Right now, he's innocent until proven guilty, and there are stations in town playing this record, and listeners requesting that we play it, and to stay competitive, I have to play it too."

R. Kelly is beloved by the African-American community in a culturally historic way, much the same as even Malcom X or Martin Luther King were in terms of their ability to lift the entire spirit of the African American people up above everyday adversity. For some of Kelly's most hard core fans, particularly his inner-city listening audience, the performer's legal challenge is not that foreign an experience from many of their own, which gains Kelly sympathy, if nothing more. Beyond that, the adversity he has so masterfully survived thus far makes him a symbol of inspiration to the aforementioned demographic in an entirely different light from the one he is traditionally admired in as an entertainer.

Using the same line of defense that President Bill Clinton did in his televised 1998 confessional regarding his sexual affair with intern Monica Lewinsky, Kelly has gone out of his way to point out in interviews that his private life is a human one, just like any of his fans. In that context, his mistakes are easier to accept because his listeners, to some degree, are prone to view him not as a larger than life super-star, but rather as a regular person with real problems.

Still, regardless of how Kelly might be humanized via the successful application of this strategy, he is still admired and beloved on another level. Because R. Kelly has lifted his fans above their every-day problems for years, so too, do they lift him up above suspicion, at least for the time being, with Kelly aiding in this process by giving fans his best new material in years.

The Chicago Tribune echoed the latter in a review of the 'Chocolate Factory', concluding that "the best of these songs—the ones with-out the legal and personal baggage attached—could keep Kelly on the airwaves for the next year while his fate is decided in court. For those who continue to support Kelly, separating his legal affairs from his musical genius will be a must in coming months. With 'Chocolate Factory' Kelly is forcing his fans to choose: Buy me (the album, the remorse, the alibis) or abandon me." His fans have obvi-ously chosen to stick by the singer.

As for those who have chosen to side against Kelly prior to his being judged one way or the other by a jury of his peers, the superstar has done his best to take the high road in lashing out against his detrac-tors, telling *Blender Magazine* in a 2003 interview that "people can say whatever they want about you without knowing the facts. They can criticize you without even knowing you and hate you when they don't even know you." By focusing on his existing fan base, and expanding on it, with hit after hit, Kelly has effectively forced a mas-sive change of tide in general public sentiment that will inevitably bleed over into the legal arena in terms of its affect on potential jurors.

Whether the wave of fan sympathy will wash Kelly's legal slate clean of his alleged sins remains unclear; what is apparent is that the singer believes in both his innocence and his higher power as fervently as he conveys in song or on stage. One thing therein is sure, that while pundits debate over the extent of art imitating life in terms of the sexual content of Kelly's music vs. his personal life, his religious conviction, also prominent throughout his music, is not part of his act.

Moreover, clearly as much a refuge for him as his music is in these troubled times, Kelly comes off as common as any other man when discussing God in his life, and perhaps feels no more important therein based on his being equally as humbled in the eyes of his creator, "There's a lot of people going through a lot of things right now that are deeper than me, you know. I see kids and people starving; a baby just died the other day from starvation. People think I'm going through something—but I know God is real. My own situation is not so heavy. We'll be all right (if we keep believing)…My mama always told me that the higher you go, you're going to pay a price…And you've got to believe that God's got your back. She told me this way back, when I was recording my second album. And I listened."

R. Kelly's belief in God's own struggle has also inspired him to keep on fighting, wherein the superstar seems to view the allegations before him very much like a competition. Kelly didn't retreat behind his legal team when the charges against him became public, rather he came out fighting, which explains his stellar year via a drive to compete with his opponent—the prosecution—on an equal level of intensity, knowing his supporters would expect nothing less.

"If you tell me on the court that we've got an hour to make a basket, I'm going to take my time. But if you tell me the pressure's on, tell me I've got two minutes, then I'm going to focus. Everything's like that with me. When I have a little pressure on me, my passion starts to feed my talent…When you're a celebrity at my level, the game gets harder. I'm in life's boxing ring. I go in there expecting to get hit. You don't train to get in there and not get hit—you take the punches. So I'm taking a few punches, but I can't think this is going to knock me out...I can't think like that."

For Kelly, being in demand, whether by the law or his fans, makes no difference in the context of his motivation to come out on top, "I'm at my best when I'm wanted...and I'm no good when I'm not. That's my kryptonite, when I'm not wanted. The (fans) showed me a lot of love (this year)." Kelly has without a doubt been an iron man this year, with a cape on his back! Not a superman but a superstar, the performer may have benefited from his adversity, if only in the sense that it brought both he and his fans back to the basics in terms of why Kelly became a legend in the first place—his talent.

As a result, Kelly is giving his fans exactly what they need to keep believing in him, and he in himself—great music, and plenty of it, "I love music, and music loves me back. We're kind of married, and I'm pregnant by music. I have three to four years' worth of work you've never heard in the vaults. I've come up with at least 20 to 25 albums."

Kelly argues that it's a lot more constructive a way to spend his time than worrying about what his detractors think of him, "I'm always in the studio—and stay busy with my music. What's the sense of hearing a lot of lies and rumors about yourself?" Kelly's rationale for keeping focused on music, rather than distracted by the controversy surrounding his case, ultimately has less to do with how that focus might benefit him in the commercial arena, and more to do with celebrating life in the fullest as long as he's permitted, by God, the law, or anyone else. He seems to believe that his fate is out of his hands, and in those of his creator, who has given him so much in life and at the same time, taken so much from him in the process—i.e. his stardom vs. his beloved mother.

By investing his money in the best lawyers, his faith in God, and his creative energy in producing the best music of his career, Kelly may very well survive the storm he faces, parting those dark clouds with his own hope; along with that, he has inspired in millions of others over his remarkable 14 year career. In the end, Kelly clearly believes his forthcoming judgment day will not be first or his last, rather just another test of his faith, which appears stronger than any superficial (i.e. mortal) conviction that might befall him, "I was raised by my mom (and taught to love) people (of) all colors, all classes, wanting to be around people and have fun. She sang…We were like best friends…She knew, she called me a genius, you know. The same thing any mama calls her son whether he has a gift or not, really. But she was always thankful for the gift of life…(Therein) I have to think good. I'm a good person. Good people think good; they think positive. That's why they *do* good."

Whether the jury's interpretation of the evidence against Kelly will come down to his motive, a crucial part of determining guilt or innocence in any criminal case, Kelly's intentions, we have to assume, were *NOT* to harm or take advantage of anyone. Anyone who has viewed the tape from which these allegations arose can see that Kelly meant to capture himself in the act of sex—this is not such a surprise, given his reputation, commercial image, and lyrical content for almost 15 years in the business.

Kelly enjoys sex, just as the rest of us do; it is human, just as he is, and as mistakes are. If Kelly made a mistake, it is fair to assume it was an honest one—engaging in sexual acts with a woman he thought was of age when she may not have in fact been. If she lied to him and he believed her, a fairly common scenario which happens to millions of Americans every year, then Kelly is guilty only of bad judgment, not of anything he should lose his freedom over, let alone the legendary and indelible mark he has made on pop music history in the course of his remarkable career…

Dedicated to the Crue:
Chris, Drew, the Sean, Alex, Adam, and Matio!

Introduction

"Every Other Time But This One..."

:**R**. Kelly loves the ladies. The ladies love R. Kelly. A potent blend of erotic, thug-laced balladry and genuine gospel-house crooning produced a sound that captured the faith of heart and hormone of millions of female fan in a single moment, setting into course a ten-year, multi-platinum run of top 40 hits saturated in one topic above all others, SEX. Robert Kelly's voice crooned seductively enough to corrupt the Virgin Mary, and while Kelly had too deep of a respect for the Lord above ever to violate the latter Mary, he certainly used his position to seduce hundreds of the former underage girls who were young enough to be virgins, and not yet old enough to legally have that chastity lifted. Kelly used his position to lift it anyway, raising hundreds of under-aged skirts over the 1990s under the guise of music rooted in a celebration of his higher power. Like many influential public figures before him who had used their position of moral righteousness as a veil behind which they indulged immoral personal fetishes—from political and civil leaders who had extramarital affairs that often produced illegitimate children, to Catholic Priests who used their religious pulpits to abuse young, impressionable alter boys, and finally pop stars like Michael Jackson, who used his God-like celebrity to indulge a similar fetish with a young, pre-teen male fan. All of the aforementioned characters were morally-conflicted individuals who were publicly adored by thousands, and sometimes, millions of fans and followers who were

1

quick to blur the lines between life and the art of entertainment and inspiration, believing their idols were like flawless diamonds in the sky that could do no wrong, when in fact their souls were internally fractured and flawed just like the everyday human. That these men had spent years and millions of dollars quietly violating the law with their indiscretions, and subsequently settling with their victims out of court for large monetary payouts, almost always in exchange for sealed testimony that could never be admitted into a criminal proceeding, further fueled the ego of their predatory nature, making them feel that much more invulnerable to persecution or prosecution. Kelly became so bold as to videotape his illegal transgressions with minors, only to have his sense of invulnerability popped when his underbelly was exposed on America's Video and DVD markets.

That he had been engaged in such transgressions came as not such a surprise as the story broke in the media like a tidal wave, carrying in its frothing surf a revelation that Kelly had settled not one but several civil suits filed by underage girls during the latter half of the 1990s, including Tracy Sampson and Tiffany Hawkins, who Kelly had taken advantage of sexually while still in their teens-, one of whom he had allegedly forced to have abort a child the affair had produced. Despite his holy water tears and proclamations that he was innocent, R. Kelly, even in admitting in defensive press interviews to not having "been a perfect man", only sounded that much more like a remorseful but belligerent and defiant Congressman Gary Condit denying a sexual affair of his own several months earlier. While their respective circumstances and professions differed, the underlying themes of betrayal of both a general public and individual admirer's trust, and of an inherent inability to face the music when trying to write their own excuse theme songs had failed, were eerily similar in nature. R. Kelly is comparable to many of history's public figures, great publicly in position, flawed privately in character. In reality, they all were very much playing roles that, while certain impressionable segments of the population bought into, no one truly could expect to be a hundred percent authentic. For example, as virile a sure thing as R. Kelly tried to come off in his songs of young lust and all-night ecstasy, he clearly had erectile malfunction in the bedroom, as evinced by his publicly bootlegged, and FBI-authenticated video taped sexual exploits. And while he saw nothing wrong with a little bump n' grind, as long as it was under aged (Kelly married the late Aaliyah at the tender age of 15 after producing her debut album), in the end he believed he could fly higher than reproach, and was knocked back down to reality by his own arrogance.

R. Kelley isn't the first celebrity to be brought down by his own home video-taped indiscretions. Rob Lowe did it ten years earlier with a pair of 16-year old fans pre-internet and before the bootleg video market was really developed as an enterprise. And while Tommy Lee and Pamela Anderson were of age, their video-taped exploits rang up over $75 million in proceeds, and became the best-selling adult entertainment video of all time, redefining the commercial value of such product. Unfortunately for R. Kelly, the Tommy Lee tape created a certain expectation among the public, and hunger among the media, that such behavior was in fact common among celebrities, and that it would only be a matter of time before the next bad boy was caught with his pants down. In this case, it was R. Kelly's misfortune to be the subject of not one, but what turned out to be numerous videos and subsequent criminal charges related to Illinois' child pornography laws. Tragic that this multi-instrumental, multi-talented performer, and writer/producer of hits for such mega-popular artists as Mary J. Blige, Whitney Houston, Celine Dion, Gladys Knight, Michael Jackson, Janet Jackson, Luther Vandross, Notorious B.I.G., Kirk Franklin, and Toni Braxton, could boast such a successful professional track record while having such a tragic personal one. As the Chicago Superintendent of Police Terry Hillard summarized the tragedy of the charges against Kelly in light of his professional successes for the media, "It's unfortunate to see Mr. Kelly's talents go to waste, but it becomes a tragedy when behavior damages the community."

Mr. Kelly's actions had not only worked to damage the community, but also his fan base, as thousands of once-adoring fans ran for cover from who one tabloid had dubbed 'Mr. (Underage) Bump N' Grind'. Radio stations like Chicago's that had once celebrated R. Kelly's catalog with repeated rotation now hosted rallies protesting the embattled pop star. He didn't help matters with the ambiguity that laced his press rebuttals to the allegations, nor by the contradictory defenses his attorneys offered—one stating that it was not Mr. Kelly at all on the tapes; another stating that even if it was Mr. Kelly, none of the women featured in sexual acts with Mr. Kelly on the tapes were underage. All this despite the fact that prior to charging Mr. Kelly, the Chicago police department had enlisted the F.B.I. to authenticate the identity of both Mr. Kelly and the alleged minor victim on the videos. The victim's aunt, who allegedly had introduced the two, went so far as to come out publicly lambasting R. Kelly in the media for taking advantage of her niece, telling MTV that she had warned the girl to "be careful…She kept coming down with me, which was [a] safe [situation] at the time. But after (Kelly). and I parted ways, it was me not watching over her. So I feel a responsibility for that also, although I'm not responsible for his actions, I feel responsible for even taking her there.…It's messed up. She's being exposed to the world. It's sickening."

Kelly himself has been largely unable to respond in-depthly to the charges lodged against him, aside from the standard "I'm innocent and being framed" rhetoric, principally because a criminal trial is pending. Instead, he has chosen to respond to the allegations that could cost him his multi-platinum career and his freedom through song, releasing a song late in the spring of 2002 entitled "Heaven I Need a Hug". While the track's title is touching, the chorus is self-pitying and uninspired, asking God for forgiveness for unspecified sins that Kelly denies having committed down here on Earth, "Heaven, I need a hug/ Is there anybody out there willing to embrace a thug?" Whether Kelly eventually owns up to his sins and repents or remains defiantly in denial of what is his fairly obvious guilt remains in question, through it is clear that he has finally begun to realize the severity of the charges now filed against him, as well as the potential weight a conviction could carry, not only in costing him his career, but also his freedom. To that end, he has begun to adopt a pattern of rhetoric in the interviews he has conducted with the press laying the groundwork for his defense, one that didn't seek to paint him as a saint, rather as a flawed man who was guilty of wrong in his life, just not this particular set of allegations, "I've done a lot of wrong things in my life, but I am not a criminal…I am not a monster that people are saying I am. And if people out there have a tape of me and they're saying it's with me and a young girl, a minor, then they're sadly mistaken or they're lying."

Unfortunately the camera rarely lies these days, and while its widely considered dumb luck to get caught on tape violating the rights of another, such as in the case of the Rodney King LAPD officers, its even dumber luck to tape yourself committing a violation of those rights. R. Kelly will inevitably have to face the music, though it won't be of his own writing, and with ambitious prosecutors composing the tune outlining his guilt, with a home-filmed music video to help sell their song, it will likely become a hit among the jurors who convict Kelly of at least some of the counts lodged against him. Kelly looks at his own life as one of giving, not one of over-indulgence. In describing his inspiration behind such R&B inspirationals like 'I Believe I Can Fly', which won him a Grammy award, Kelly described his songwriting gift as something that "did a lot of people some good…(made) us all feel like we can all love… that song had no color." As touching as Kelly's goal toward eliminating boundaries with and through his music was, he went too far in his interpretation of what lines were acceptable to blur. Race, yes. Age, no. In music, one unfortunately has a natural tendency to transcend the other, and because adulation doesn't discriminate, Kelly didn't either, reciprocally reaching out to his fans with an open-armed policy that invited girls of any age into his fan club, and ultimately into his bedroom. Kelly admitted as much in terms of his desire for a universal musical appeal when he described his sound as one in which ""I want [listeners] to feel that they can reach out and touch me, call me whenever. I want them to feel like they can touch the sky, leap over the moon. I want them to feel like they can accomplish their goals...I want them to just feel free." Free to open themselves sexually to Kelly, or 'Daddy' as he liked to be called on his now infamous home video taped exploits, in turn leaving Kelly free to sow his royal R&B oats in the Garden of Eden with a very young Eve.

Ultimately, R. Kelly has two courts to face, that of the legal system, and of public opinion. America can be forgiving to its celebrities when they commit certain wrongs—domestic violence, drug addiction, and even sex with a minor where the star clearly didn't know the age—unfortunately for R. Kelly, he targeted his victims with a fetish for that very fact, their under-18 status. Whether a fetish he has had since a childhood, or one that he developed as an up and coming R&B star, R. Kelly clearly has an illness. He has discussed his upbringing as one that was rough...but it was fair...(and) got me where I am today mentally." That is a problem. And one that hopefully will be addressed through court-ordered therapy in the course of whatever sentence Kelly receives upon being found guilty of his violation of the public's trust, and of Illinois' child pornography laws. In viewing the video that brought reality crashing down upon R. Kelly, he is shown in the beginning of the tape clearly testing his position, bouncing up and down upon a cushion before the camera, to ensure his acts would clearly be captured. This demonstrates premeditation, which, coupled with his motive, to indulge a sick fetish, clearly convicts Kelly in the eyes of any unbiased, sensible viewer. Unfortunately for Kelly, there have now been thousands upon thousands of them as that many of his home videos were distributed for sale on the bootleg market, and in some cases, in legitimate music chains throughout the country.

Now, as the American public awaits the start of what is sure to be a sensational trial, with juicy revelations about the private life of this very public R&B star, and a media frenzy that is sure to keep the details of Kelly's illegal exploits in the national papers for months, and the tabloids for even longer, we are left to wonder—who is R. Kelly, behind the music, behind the videos, and behind the persona his pop stardom creates? His talent is fascinating, his climb to the top of the charts equally so. Now, we begin to explore the past of R. Kelly in the hopes of uncovering the truth behind his denials concerning his penchant for exploiting young women on video tape for private gratification, the rationale which explains why such a publicly celebrated pop star could have such a conflicted private life, and most importantly, what circumstances in R. Kelly's past led him so carelessly to this point of both public and private reckoning. *Your Body's Calling Me* is the story of the life and times of R. Kelly.

Chapter 1

"I Wish"

Architecture, racism and even good intentions have conspired to create poverty in Chicago's housing projects... Some 95% of CHA residents are on some kind of public assistance, compared with roughly 25% in New York. Predictably, CHA buildings are magnets for drugs and crime...Chicago's special problems were born in the 1950s when local politicians, including the mayor, Richard J. Daley, began to use public housing to segregate the city's Rapidly growing black Population. Meanwhile, city builders had become enamored of Le Corbusier's vision of urban buildings as 'islands in the sky'. The result was hulking high-rises in poor black neighborhoods, the worst of which is an uninterrupted four-mile stretch of public housing in the city's Southside...**Out of all this came a musical genius, a musician beyond beautiful.**

Robert L. Kelly was born on January 8, 1967. His family settled in the Hyde Park-section of the South Side of Chicago, Illinois when Kelly was still an infant. The third of four children, including two brothers, Carry and Bruce, and a sister, Teresa, Robert was raised by a single mother, Joanne Kelly, a teacher and devout Baptist who later became a Born-Again Christian. Young Robert first lived with his family in the housing projects on 63rd Street before moving to a small house at 107th Street and Parnell Avenue on Chicago's South Side.

Kelly grew up like many of America's inner city African Americans, without a father for the majority of his childhood. Kelly has not commented much on his childhood, other than to categorize it as "rough…but it got me mentally to where I am today." Kelly as a youth was extremely close to his mother, often running to her for shelter from his two older brothers' teasing. Kelly preferred his mother's company to most others as an adolescent, telling *Vibe Magazine* in an interview that, "He enjoyed eavesdropping on his mother, aunt, and sister as they gossiped at the kitchen table as much as he enjoyed playing basketball with his brothers on the playground." It has been additionally rumored in the media that Kelly suffered abuse at the hands of an older man in his neighborhood at a young age, and that this abuse fueled his preference for his mother's company over that of his male siblings and peers.

Despite the protection he felt he received by staying constantly close to his mother, Kelly was raised among the same type of narcotics-fueled and gang-related violence that has plagued America's inner cities for years. Kelly has often told in interviews of one of his earliest exposures to the more savage side of the urban jungle in which he was reared involving his being shot at the age of 13 while trying to resist the attempts of several thugs to steal his Huffy bicycle outside of the notorious Ida B. Wells housing project development. Sadly, it has been reported since that his mother, Joanne, told a close acquaintance on her death bed that her beloved son had fabricated the robbery story to cover up a suicide attempt. No matter the circumstance behind the shooting, in the end, Kelly lost a piece of his innocence, that was traded for a bullet fragment that still resides lodged in his shoulder to this day. As his high school music teacher and mentor at the Kenwood Academy, Lena McLin recalled the state of the Kelly home during Robert's childhood, the degree of poverty that he was reared in was frightening, "It was bare. One table, two chairs. There was no father there, I knew that, and they had very little."

Kelly coped via the same refuge as many of America's inner city African American males—playing basketball. Initially envisioning basketball as his escape from the poverty of his childhood, Kelly honed his skills on the same courts that produced such NBA greats as Washington Wizards' star Juwan Howard and Miami Heat star Tim Hardaway, whose father was the playground basketball legend Donald Hardaway. As Juwan Howard described his upbringing on the same streets and courts as Kelly, it was his dream of going pro in the NBA that helped him survive his impoverished childhood such that, "Some would look at my childhood and say 'That kid doesn't stand a chance.' I was poor and wasn't raised by two loving parents." Fortunately for Kelly he had a pair of guardian Angels watching over his life's direction, one being his mother, the other being Lena McLin.

While it wasn't until high school that Kelly would discover the depth of his talent for music, much of the roots of his sound's influence can be traced to his home life. His mother raised Kelly in a spiritual house filled with the God-fearing, Soul, and Rhythm and Blues sounds of artists including Stevie Wonder, Marvin Gaye, the Isley Brothers, and Donny Hathaway—all of whose influence would hold resonance for Kelly in the adolescence that would follow and out of which he would develop his own erotic, Gospel-laced R&B sound.

If Kelly's mother had laid the foundations of his interest in music and birth of his talent by raising him in a melodious home, it was his music teacher at the Kenwood Academy, Lena McLin, whom he has referred to as "my second mother," who brought him out of his cocoon and should be most prominently credited with developing Kelly's musical genius. McLin, herself the niece of the legendary father of Gospel music, Thomas A. Dorsey, recognized Kelly's raw musical talent when he was barely a teen, and took him under her wing for the next few years, recalling that it was not difficult to pick young Robert out of a class full of teens as a musical standout with the potential to become something very special, so much that when she first heard him sing, "You always know. You just do." McLin remembered Kelly's vocal talent as something that touched people differently even at the tender age of 14, "Just a child…So rich in voice. [I couldn't] believe that [was] just a child?…God trot on my heart that he was a genius, a Stevie Wonder."

McLin believed so thoroughly in Kelly's musical potential that she felt its importance and his subsequent need to focus exclusively on it clearly outweighed that of Robert's passion for basketball, such that she had him bounced off the team. As McLin mentored Kelly, she got to know him more and more personally, wherein she described his personality during this crucial period of adolescence as ,"Respectful, shy sometimes. He was not the troublemaker." McLin taught her students in Bel Canto, an operatic style of singing which emphasized an evenness of tone and vocal precision.

According to the instructor, Kelly also received a thorough education in the fundamentals of Music Theory which included, "music history, theory, piano, choir, opera workshop, jazz workshop— Robert took it all." While young Robert was initially shy to his talents, McLin took it upon herself to coax him out of the shadow of his own insecurity by factoring the inspiration of religion into Kelly's motivation toward being outwardly pursuant of his musical abilities, again reinforcing the roots of his fusion of gospel themes into his erotic R&B sound. As McLin recalled, if Robert was at first "Ashamed of [himself musically], I'd make [him] stand in front of the mirror…I asked [him], 'Do you think God made a mistake? He could've made you a roach!'"

Kelly became bolder with his music talent as the years went on, his turning point being a year-end high school talent contest where Robert wore a suit and sunglasses and performed a stirring rendition of the Stevie Wonder classic "Ribbon in the Sky." As he became more comfortable with his identity as a musician and performer, McLin took it upon herself to broaden Kelly's musical pallet beyond the boundaries of her classroom, taking the student with her to a music educator's conference in Austria among other musical extra-curriculars.

Kelly, in looking back years later, remarked to one journalist that he regarded McLin as "my pastor and my second mother. She's the lady who picked me out of 50 people in the class and told me I was going to be a big recording artist...She's everything to me. She took me under her wing in high school. She told me I would be a big star. She used to always tell me that. She really pushed me, and she's still pushing me. She told me back then I would work with Michael Jackson, and it came to be." Concerning the roots of Kelly's fetish for young girls, McLin recalls no time during which young Robert displayed anything other than the professionalism of a determined talent on his way up and out of the childhood poverty that surrounded him. In short, as McLin saw it, Kelly was all business while in the classroom, "I don't know what he did outside of school. But in the school, there was no hanky panky."

Though Kelly would never graduate from the Kenwood Academy largely due to poor grades in most academic subjects outside of music, he had become an accomplished classical pianist, and had developed a refined vocal range that allowed him to alternate easily from baritone to alto. Additionally, Kelly had composed upward of 500 songs of his own, many of which McLin insisted Kelly copyright along the way. As his musical mentor and surrogate guardian would tell *Vibe Magazine* in an interview years later in reflection on Kelly's musical talent and its continued potential to grow and reach new plateaus and ears, "We've not yet seen the heights to which Robert can go...Robert is an immense talent. I don't say that to build him up, I say it because I know what's there. Where he chooses to go with it is his decision." Where he chose to go following his departure prematurely from the Kenwood Academy was to the streets, not to hustle narcotics, but rather his music to the morning commuters on Chicago's L metro-transit rail.

Looking back on Kelly's impoverished childhood, one can't help but feel a measure of sympathy for the embattled R&B star. An examination of one of Kelly's ballads, "I Wish," recorded in honor of his mother following her death, reveals a man in deep personal turmoil over his childhood still coming to grips with its pain in the midst of an appreciation for the woman whose love helped see him through to this point. As revealed in the song's lyrics, Kelly not only reaches up toward his mother, but also out to his estranged sister and to a deceased childhood friend whose death Kelly is still mourning.

While R. Kelly found refuge from the pain of his past in his music, he also discovered a veil for unfettered access to excess, and in embracing the dual themes of religion and eroticism in his music, Kelly created a natural paradox within his public persona, and arguably within himself. While he managed a bit of introspection on the latter ten years into his career, for the first decade, Kelly would make a name for himself as R&B's most prolific purveyor of sexual Pop anthems, representing to R&B in the 1990s what Prince had been to the 1980s. As captured in terms of its true intent in a review at NME.com, Kelly's "I Wish," released in 2000, offered listeners his most revealing glimpse into what was still unresolved within R. Kelly's past, and most importantly, possibly what he intended to work toward through his music in the future, "While Kelly fights the burdens of fame on "I Wish," he also speaks of the pain he endures having survived his deceased mother and his realization that leaving poverty has lead to a wealthy isolation...(With) emotive clarity, Kelly reveals his survivor's guilt at outliving a childhood friend, all of which prove that when he shelves his obsession with opening your legs and opens his mind, that he is capable of making thought-provoking material."

R. Kelly, ten years earlier, was hungry for a shot at stardom and had only two things on his mind—getting to the top and finessing as many young ladies as he could on the way there. An examination of R. Kelly's roots as a performer serves to reveal much about the roots of his fetish for young women, and how the two intertwined to lay the foundations for both his rise to the top of the charts, as well as for his potential downfall from that position.

Chapter 2

"Born Into the 1990s"

No one has ever seriously regarded R. Kelly as thug material. Though he grew up in the projects on the South Side of Chicago, he made his name as a silky R&B sexual crooner, which, given his current predicament, has caused some to classify him as a pervert, but never a thug. Nevertheless, R. Kelly did begin his music career on the streets of Chicago, not as a drug dealer or a gang member, but rather as a street musician performing first for change before droves of subway commuters beneath Chicago's L metro line in the late 1980s.

As Kelly, himself, has painted the portrait of his roots as an R&B performer, becoming a professional musician was never his intention, "Well, it started out as me and my boys just messing around performing on the streets." In fact, it was not Kelly, but one of his friends, who first put an entrepreneurial slant on Kelly's musical talents, inviting Chicago's morning commuters to compliment Kelly's performances with more than just their applause. According to Kelly, as it happened "one of the fellows dropped a hat while I was playing this keyboard and people started putting money in it. That became our thing. I simply made a regular job out of it."

Kelly, like most struggling musicians was, in the beginning, content with just being in the position to make a living playing his music.

However, as word began to spread locally, Kelly became more and more the star attraction of Chicago's L Metro street musicians. As his audience grew, beat cops were often summoned to break up the crowds, and Kelly more than once was cited for performing in public without a permit, among any number of other trivial, misdemeanor infractions of city ordinances. Despite his warnings, the attention and income Kelly was receiving only made him bolder, such that as Kelly recalled, "The hat started getting full really quick…Suddenly it wasn't a job anymore. So [every] day I'm down there again with my keyboard and a bucket. I made $400 in about six hours."

Catching on that his musical talents were in fact marketable to a paying audience, Kelly began to hone his performance skills to accompany his already-developed musical chops. One of Kelly's first moves was to form a group of musicians to back him and several dancers with the vision in mind of moving from the street corner to the stage. The result was the assembled of his first group, MGM, launched in 1989. Against a musical backdrop that mixed Hip-Hop, R&B, and Dance, R. Kelly attempted to refine his sound, which embodied the likes of Stevie Wonder, Marvin Gaye, and the Isley Brothers as its root, to reflect a balance of the harder-edged R&B material of solo stars like Bobby Brown and Keith Sweat with the more traditional, Gospel-rooted, soul sounds of Luther Vandross and the Winans. In seeking to achieve a middle-road in which he could serve both his maker and his hormones simultaneously, Kelly was methodically creating his own brand of erotic, Gospel-laced R&B which would take over the masses in a few short years.

Kelly's early prospects with MGM looked promising. In addition to establishing a solid performance reputation in and around Chicago's club scene, R. Kelly succeeded in landing a spot on the Star Search-esque television show Big Break, hosted by Natalie Cole, daughter of legendary soul crooner Nat King Cole, in the later part of 1989. Among a handful of other talented finalists, Kelly's group took home the top honors, including a $100,000 prize, and MGM seemed headed toward stardom. Unfortunately, things did not take off the way Kelly had expected them to and he was stuck back at square one after breaking the group up at the end of the decade.

It was clear at the time to Kelly that he had the raw musical talent hit songwriting prowess, and a strong on-stage performing presence to make it. What he lacked were the right connections to properly showcase and shop his sound around to prospective label A&R executives. Rather than begin the process of assembling another group, Kelly made the decision to try his luck as a solo performer, diversifying his palette to make room for more performance options toward his dream of becoming a star. One of those added avenues turned out to be the lucky break R. Kelly had been looking for. It came while he was auditioning for a musical at the Regal Theatre in Chicago and caught the eye of veteran music Manager Barry Hankerton who was at the time the husband of R&B legendary Songstress Gladys Knight.

Barry Hankerton had been a presence in and around the entertainment business for years. He had worked both in a managerial capacity as president of Blackground Enterprises, and had experience as an agent, A&R executive, and as a producer. Kelly not only caught his eye, but also his ear and his business interest, quickly signing Kelly to an exclusive management contract in 1990. In addition to his performance potential as a solo artist, Hankerton was equally as eager to invest in Kelly's abilities as a songwriter and producer, which traditionally has held a more lasting and lucrative resonation in the record business. To that end, Hankerton put Kelly to work writing and producing demos for a number of the acts Hankerton managed. (In a strange twist of fate, it would be his manager who would introduce Kelly to his first bride a short 3 years later when the hot new crooner/producer was brought in to work on a demo for Hankerton's niece, Aaliyah, managed under Hankerton's Blackground Enterprises umbrella alongside Kelly.)

To couple with the break Kelly had received by hooking up with Hankerton, that same year in the summer of 1990, R. Kelly would catch the biggest break of his career, when he performed impromptu for guests at a friend's barbecue, one of whom happened to include Jive Records' A&R Executive and Talent Scout, Wayne Williams. In the classic tradition of being in the right place at the right time, much like Sony's president Tommy Matolla's instinctual decision to sign Mariah Carey only an hour after meeting her at a party and hearing her demo tape, Williams made a similar decision in nature by giving Kelly as much as a verbal record deal on the spot.

When Hankerton was later brought in to negotiate the finer points, including setting Kelly up with his own publishing company on the outset of the deal (in which Hankerton, of course, had a financial interest), and all the ink had dried, Jive Records would be the cocoon out of which one of the biggest R&B stars of the 1990s would soon thereafter hatch. As Williams recalled his first encounter with Kelly's silky-smooth voice and charismatic presence as a performer, he knew he had struck gold before Kelly's first single would ever hit that mark on its way to platinum, "He was singing original material and he had dance steps to match...You had to be impressed."

In was the dawn of a new decade, and a new sound referred to as New Jack Swing, which embodied punchy, street-savvy beats with sexually energetic melodies and Poppy choruses flavored the streets. While the tempo typically favored racier numbers in the vein of Bel Biv Devoe's "Poison" and Bobby Brown's Teddy Reily-produced, gangsta-love formula best captured in edgy, top-ten hits like "My Perogative," the early 1990s version of top-forty friendly R&B also allowed room for slower dance numbers by artists like Keith Sweat, Ralph Tresvant, and Johnny Gill, as well as four-part harmonies by a new brand of groups emerging, including Guy, Jodeci, and Boys to Men. A&R executives from established R&B-oriented labels like Jive Records, Uptown Entertainment, and Tommy Boy Records were on the lookout like vultures for new meat, viewing the next wave of prospective R&B sex symbols through the same eyes as the millions of teenage girls they hoped to sell this new generation of new jack superstars to. Out of this new sound, which blended soulful vocals with Hip-Hop rhythm tracks all the while staying true to a R&B/Soul foundation, R. Kelly's next attempt at group success, Public Announcement, was born.

Following the fold of MGM, R. Kelly had regrouped, focused on further honing and establishing his credentials as a solo artist, and in the process, as a songwriter and producer. Though Kelly had signed officially with Jive Records in late 1990, it would be a full year and a half before his first album, Born into the 90s, would be released in 1992. However, there was no downtime during that period, nor was Kelly working solely on his own debut. Instead, he was building capital with his new label as a producer for some of Jive Records and its subsidiary labels' biggest hits in the early part of the decade.

Among Kelly's other early hits in the course of collaborating with other artists, he achieved chart success with Hi-Five, whose number one single, "Quality Time," that R. Kelly co-wrote and produced. As Kelly's career-resume expanded, between 1991 and 1993 alone, he worked in a composing, and/or producing capacity with such legends as Gladys Knight (manager Hankerton's now-ex wife), David Peaston, and most notably at the time, the Winans gospel clan, with whom he produced and performed a duet, "That Extra Mile" with Ronald Winans. Despite his success behind the scenes with the latter artists, R. Kelly's debut as a solo artist would be the biggest highlight of his still fledgling, yet already accomplished, resume.

To that end, in the spring of 1992, R. Kelly released his debut LP, Born Into the 90s with his band Public Announcement. Embodying a sound which critics described as, "A mix of soul, swing beats infused with Rap and pure attitude," Kelly's sound, "Created a smooth, professional mixture of Hip-Hop beats, Soul-man crooning, and Funk, the most distinctive element of Kelly's music [being] its explicit carnality."

If Kelly's critics were taken aback by his ability to be commercial while in the same time sexually suggestive in a way that would have only been embraced by the R&B underground prior thereto, his record label was equally, if not more, shocked at the instant smash that Kelly's debut LP proved to be, certified platinum within the first few months of its release, and spawning the top ten R&B smashes "She's Got that Vibe" and "Slow Dance (Hey Mr. DJ)," as well as the top 40 crossover smashes "Honey Love" and "Dedicated." By the end of 1992, Born into the 90s had become Jive Records' third best selling R&B title of the year. Though Kelly's career was taking off at the time, he remained extremely humble in his personal life, living in a one-bedroom high rise apartment, indulging himself only in a gold Toyota Land Cruiser, and joking to one journalist at the time that, "I'm more experienced at not having money...I'm better at not handling it."

By the decade's end, R. Kelly would, according to *Billboard Magazine*, rack up 15 Top 40 hits, surpassing all of his genre counterparts as a solo artist. Moreover, Kelly ended up in the top ten's top ten, racking up 8 Top Ten smashes in Billboard's Top 200 list. Perhaps even more impressive, his role as collaborative composer and producer with other artists would expand outside of his R&B genre, reflecting the diversity of Kelly's talents, as he crafted hits for many of the world's biggest Pop stars, including Michael Jackson, Celine Dion, Notorious BIG, Puffy, Janet Jackson, Toni Braxton, Mary J. Blige, NAS, Maxwell, Kirk Franklin, and KC & Jo Jo.

It was Kelly's aforementioned knack for generating cross-genre hits that would first bring him into contact in 1992 with his most - personally invested collaboration—with his manager Barry Hankerton's niece, Aaliyah. The chemistry between the two extended almost immediately beyond the professional level as they secretly married in August, 1994. This would serve as the first public evidence of Kelly's tendency toward and involvement with underage women and act as a forecast for a pattern of abusive indulgence and subsequent trouble that would result for Kelly as his career skyrocketed in the first half of the 1990s.

Sadly, the aforementioned pattern of abuse would begin well before Kelly was a superstar, dating back to late 1990, when he was still a newly signed artist in development at Jive Records, writing and recording his debut album with supporting group Public Announcement. As part of R. Kelly's image-building as an up and coming R&B star, it was important to the singer from the early stages to reflect what was in essence a genuine social conscience—to give back to the inner city communities which had helped to mold him. Sadly, beneath the veil of a charitable agenda, he was simultaneously laying the groundwork for what would eventually become Kelly's dangerously reckless routine of seducing underage women who looked up to the R&B star as a mentor.

While Kelly would abuse his position with impressionable teens time and again to indulge his sexual fantasies, he did commit himself to a fairly regular schedule of volunteer appearances and activities involving young children who came from the same impoverished, inner-city circumstance and up-bringing as he had, in the hopes of somehow inspiring or encouraging their eventual growth out of that predicament. Toward that end, Kelly visited his alma mater, the Kenwood Academy in Hyde Park, Chicago, during 1991 to speak before the class of his beloved former music instructor, Lena McLin. It was in the course of that visit that Kelly met freshman choir girl Tiffany Hawkins, who was at the time 14 years of age. The two would go on to begin a relationship that would, in its early stages, not address Hawkins' virginity, but still would involve other sexual contact. Kelly wasn't only interested in Hawkins, as he soon befriended one of her classmates and fellow choir girl, who recalls both she and Hawkins' awe at the time to be the subject of the up and coming R&B star's interest in them, "We were ugly little girls compared to what he could have had." Still, the girls, young, naive, impressionable, and both with professional musical aspirations, took eagerly to Kelly's advances.

Establishing an MO, and a blueprint for the process by which Kelly would recruit his teenage subjects of seduction in the years to come, Hawkins' classmate and fellow seducee recall that, at first, the singer was "real sweet, like a big brother." As much as Kelly was clearly the aggressor in his pursuit of the young girls from Kenwood Academy with whom he had some of his first documented underage sexual trysts, Hawkins' classmate, who, to this day, has chosen to remain anonymous when going on record, acknowledges that both she and Hawkins played at least a supporting role in following Kelly's lead, such that she claims in retrospect to "blame myself as much as I blame him. Even though I was young, I knew what I was doing."

Still, as 1991 continued into 1992, both girls began hanging out with Kelly through all-night recording sessions at the Chicago Recording Company, and their relations with Kelly began to take on more advanced sexual definitions, as Hawkins and her classmate began to genuinely feel that there interaction with Kelly might bear some musical fruit. Both believed this in part because Kelly made it clear that he was in such a position, communicating to both girls that he could make them protégés.

Kelly, while enticing the girls into a more intensified sexual relationship, baited them along with gifts and a Mr. Nice-Guy routine that often, according to Hawkins' classmate, included "anything we asked for, but we weren't going to ask for much—a pair of Air

Jordans or $100 was a lot of money to us…He treated us very well." As Kelly's affair with Hawkins and her classmate intensified, they, as documented in Hawkins' 1996 lawsuit, had sex with other under-age girls in his apartments at 9 S. Wabash, 185 N. Harbor Dr, and other locations in Chicago. Though Kelly's relationship with Hawkins allegedly simmered down in the spring of 1993, prior to his marriage to a then-15 year old Aaliyah, the R&B star did begin to utilize Hawkins and her choir mate in the recording studio where Kelly would "say things like 'I can make you a star' all the time."

Kelly eventually convinced both girls to drop out of Kenwood Academy well before they were eligible for graduation to work full-time for Kelly. In essence, by doing so, Kelly had made both women employees, and had made himself their employer, putting himself in an even more vulnerable position for possible future litigation should he have a falling out with either of the two women. As Hawkins' classmate remembers, Kelly at the time was insistent that both girls needed to be in his service full-time, telling them, "'If you want to be serious about the music, you have to be at the studio and not at school, because school isn't going to make you a millionaire.'"

To his credit, Kelly did utilize Hawkins' choir mate's vocal talents in a back-up capacity while recording Aaliyah's debut LP while continuing to heighten the intensity of the pair's sexual encounters, often involving third parties. Hawkins confirmed this in her 1996 civil deposition wherein she recalled that by 1993 her relationship with Kelly had taken on a less desirable, and even less voluntary for that matter, tone wherein Kelly "'required her to have sex with him'…as a basis for employment…and also made her 'participate in…group sexual intercourse' [with] other underage girls."

As Kelly's career began to skyrocket with the success of his debut LP, Born into the 90s, he continued his relationships with both girls, employing them in a full-time capacity and, according to his Kenwood cuties, expanding his roster of sexual partners to include other underage women who, as both later testified to on record, also participated in group sex in Kelly's studio, among other places, to satisfy the singer's sexual requests. In the course of one such tryst, Hawkins' classmate recalled that she once had sex with him while he simultaneously fondled Hawkins who was age 15 at the time.

In the end, Kelly appeared to have been doing nothing more than playing an elaborate game of tease, leading both girls on for the better part of their adolescence by waving the promise of a genuine chance at stardom before each woman's eyes in exchange for fulfilling Kelly's sexual indulgences and engaging in a careless pattern of disregard for their own welfare along the way. In hindsight, Hawkins' classmate and fellow Kelly-victim feels a mix of regret and sympathy for what, in the end, was the R&B star's blatant manipulation of both women, "He hurt me by not helping me out and telling me to drop out of school. He told me and Tiffany both...At 16, that's like a dream to us to work with R. Kelly, so we listened to him...I think it's a sickness."

During the period following the release of Born Into the 90s, and later in 1993, his solo debut, Kelly would begin his professional and personal collaboration with Aaliyah in the spring of 1994, which would take on a very different tone from his other underage trysts. As Kelly became emotionally involved with the fledgling R&B diva, he secretly battled to keep his two worlds hidden from one another while he continued to indulge both, toward the same hollow end—manipulating underage women. Kelly, however, would seek in the future to distinguish his relationship with Aaliyah from any other involvement on his part with minors, attempting to draw a fine line between love and lust.

Chapter 3

"Bump N' Grind"

Though R. Kelly's career was only two years old in 1993, and should, by industry standards, have still been fledgling, his status as an overnight superstar felt as natural to R&B fans as his music did to their ears. Kelly was a breed apart from the one-hit wonder formula that had dominated the early 1990s New Jack movement, principally because he defied that label by continually producing hits. Additionally, Kelly was drawing ready comparisons to Prince based on his extraordinary talents both on stage and in the studio behind the boards. Not only could he dazzle audiences of screaming women night after night, but he also dazzled record executives with his ability to compose and produce top-10 hits as well as play the majority of their instrumentation single-handedly.

Kelly was a true Pop prodigy, but the mystery of his talent went beyond conventional pondering. He had no mentor that could be publicly identified, as fellow R&B crossover phenomenon Michael Jackson had in his early years with Barry Gordy and Quincy Jones, nor did he have a distinctive root in one musical style. Rather, Kelly blended both theme and rhythm into a perfect Pop medium that allowed him to cross the musical map from gospel to funk, from the church to the bedroom, all within the same time and song.

From Kelly's point of view, the varying and often conflicting lyrical content of his songs were, in the end, all bound through the chameleon-like musical foundation that laid beneath each seductive or soul-searching track, such that, according to Kelly, " [If you] take away the sexy bump and grind, you can easily put in gospel lyrics." The secret to Kelly's immediate and massive crossover success laid in his ability to construct instrumental tracks that were irresistible to any confessing ear. Whether in the context of a prayer to God or a profession of desire, Kelly had built his own temple of erotic devotion and millions of young, impressionable women were coming to worship.

As such, by the winter of 1993, R. Kelly's career as a solo artist was in full flourish. His debut solo LP "12 Play" was released in November, following his group Public Announcement's debut Born in the 90s. Certified platinum by the early spring, and triple platinum by the summer of 1994, Kelly had quickly begun to distinguish himself from the mediocre pool of R&B leftovers from the late 1980s, like Bobby Brown, whose follow-ups to smash hits like "Don't Be Cruel" were under-performing. As well, he stood apart from the newer crop of recruits, like Color Me Badd and Silk who were turning out to be one-hit wonders as R&B was still finding its commercial footing in the early part of the new decade. As a result, Kelly was, in essence, charting a new course for top forty R&B hits by creating his own genre of crossover: one that perfectly mixed the traditional components of an R&B hit with a new sexual boldness that did away with the need for subtly. Kelly's sound was uninhibited, erotically timed to perfection, vocally precise in conviction, and too rhythmically smooth for any listening ear to resist, such that, the freedom he created in his process allowed Kelly to musically soar, taking his career right along for the ride.

Kelly's sound was distinct due to its ability to blend what one reviewer at the time called "cutting edge, street-wise Hip-Hop music and storytelling with smooth love songs." That formula would help to push 12 Play to platinum status by the end of the year, producing international top-40 hits with "Your Body's Callin," "Sex Me (Parts I and II)," "She's Got That Vibe," and the album's biggest smash, which would go on to revolutionize R&B's crossover and become Kelly's signature concert smash, "Bump 'n Grind." "Bump 'n' Grind" remained at number one for longer than any other R&B single of the 30 years prior.

On stage, Kelly was dubbed by *Ebony Magazine* as "The 'Prince of Pillowtalk' who dropped his pants during his concerts to the delight of thousands of screaming women." Kelly's label, Jive Records, took Kelly very seriously as not just a musician, but also as a potential sexual icon from the outset of his career, marketing him in a manner reminiscent of the male Pop crooner superstars of the late 1950s and 1960s, such that, as one label executive Wayne Williams reasoned, "Elvis had a magnetism about him with women, and Rob [Kelly] has it too...He's a star [of that stature]."

According to Kelly, his philosophy for capturing the intensity of his recorded music on-stage involved achieving a mirrored intensity between the onstage delivery and the audience receipt, such that his largest challenge was to make every show feel special to the fans who show out to see Kelly, "Sometimes every stage looks the same. But when you hit the stage, everything lights up. You've got to really love this profession to get with it, and I really love this...I [don't do] a lot of interviews [on the road] because the show takes a lot of concentration. It takes a lot of energy. Rest and total concentration are necessary. Every show I look at like a championship game."

On the stage, Kelly made sure the crowd had fun, but offstage, Kelly was all business with his large entourage of nearly 20, explaining to one journalist, "I try to make everyone in my entourage do some kind of work. If you're going to go with me [on the road], you're going to do something. There's no dead meat...I just like to see the people with me working. When we go to the mall, I want them to be able to buy something on their own. I don't want them to be looking at me. So I give them a job." Kelly undoubtedly felt a raw connection to his fans that only could have been achieved through a hard work that garnered a legitimate intimacy and connection between himself and his crowd, such that, according to Kelly, "It feels…good to know you got people depending on you to come out with a song that's going to make them want to make love, have a party, or get up on the floor when its time to dance. You start to feel like that's your responsibility."

In elaborating on his formula for satisfying the desires of his largely-female audience who he described as recipients of "my passion, [my] sexual abilities," Kelly clearly views the live performance of his music as the fruit of a tree whose roots begin in the studio, where, as Kelly explained jokingly to one journalist, "I become very horny and lonely in the studio and [take] it all out in my music." More seriously elaborating on his composing/producing methodology, Kelly described himself as "an in-the-basement, weird-science kind of guy when it comes to my music. I like to work in my laboratory in the middle of the night when the world seems asleep. That's how I come up with my own twisted ideas, my little schemes, my little hooks…I and my music have an understanding. I never get in its way. I let it breathe. I never hassle it or force it to do anything. That way we will stay married."

With his first solo album, 12 Play, Kelly had gone out on a long limb in an attempt to redefine what was, at the time, considered cutting-edge in R&B, such that, in seeking to raise the bar "I was really taking a chance with the concept of this album…I really didn't know if the album would be as successful as its been, but I hoped that it would be…I recorded 12 Play the way I did because of how I was feeling at that time."

Kelly's gamble had paid off handsomely, rewarding him with the complete confidence and support of his record label and allowing him the artistic freedom to expand his pallet from that of a solo artist to a collaborator; a transition rooted both in his talent and his work ethic. As Kelly would explain concerning his legendary work schedule in the early portion of his career, his drive was motivated by a combination of creative energy and hunger to escape the poverty that had dictated his entire childhood, so much so that at times he worked around the clock in the studio "like I ain't never had a bite to eat, like I ain't never had a dollar in my pocket…working my butt off, but never knowing I'm tired…There have been times when I have been up three or four days straight working on this music. But didn't know it, didn't want to know it, didn't care."

With Kelly's commercial success, word began to quickly spread throughout the industry. One journalist recalled at the time that "music insiders like Griff Morris, executive director of the Chicago chapter of the National Academy of Arts and Sciences, says Kelly's work ethic 'has become legendary. Almost everyone in the business knows about his all-night recording sessions. His commitment to music is awesome.'"

As artists, managers, and label heads began to take notice, Kelly responded in interview after interview by attempting to define his sound as broader than the genre he had been marketed in up to that point, both in an effort to expand his fan base and to let artists know in and beyond R&B that he had a talent capable of formatting itself successfully to any genre for the purposes of collaboration, "I like to come with concepts…When I create a song for myself or another artist, I see the entire thing—what the song should be like, how it should be produced, how the video should look, the image of the artist for the single—it's a package deal." In explaining why his music would naturally appeal to a boundless audience, Kelly cited a love for his songs that was genuinely heart-felt, such that, by his formula, he nurtured every note of every composition with a theme in mind that was universal in its message and impact, sowing all listeners together with the common thread of conviction, regardless of the subject matter, "I love the music that I make…and I believe that's why other people love it. Because whatever comes from the heart reaches the heart, whether good or bad. Sometimes it may not be as good as it should be…but if its reality—whether it's sexual or whether its religious or believing in yourself—then that's what I'll sing about."

In further defending himself to critics, including his success being ignored by both the American Music Awards and the Grammys, Kelly argued that "people are allowed to think what they want, and I have a right to sing about what I want…I wouldn't say my music is raunchy—just sexually aware. Criticizing me is like criticizing the evening news for showing what's really going on." Kelly's philosophy and message was received and affirmed by listeners at radio stations with number one record after record, peaking with the smash success of 12 Play's biggest hit, "Bump N Grind," which made chart history in 1994 as the longest running Number One R&B single in Billboard chart history. Kelly's success as a recording artist and live performer allowed him to take his act internationally to the United Kingdom in 1994, increasing his broadening appeal to R&B fans worldwide.

Still, despite his natural onstage magnetism and growing seasoning as a performer, Kelly acknowledged having the "butterflies syndrome" common among many multi-platinum performers, commenting that "a lot of times (when I'm performing), I do tend to get little shakes in my pants." Nevertheless, very little stood in R. Kelly's way as his stardom continued to rise into 1994 beyond expectations anyone at that point was willing to set for him, namely because up unto that point, Kelly had made history defying all that had been placed before him. As an album, 12 Play's chart success for a debut made history. In December of 1993, the album's first single "Sex Me (Parts I & II)" was certified gold and by March of 1994, the album's seminal single, "Bump N' Grind" was certified platinum and had hit number 1 on both the Billboard Top 200 Singles chart, and the

Billboard R&B/Hip-Hop Singles chart. Kelly's fortunes richened in the summer of 1994 when his third single, "Your Body's Calling," hit the Billboard Top 10 and was certified Gold while its parent album, 12 Play, was certified triple platinum.

Amid all of his success, Kelly was no stranger to the party scene and he made sure to sow his wild oats while riding the tidal waves of success during the early years of his career between 1991 and 1994. It was during this period that Kelly began to develop a reputation for a preference toward underage women—behavior that he sought time and again in later years to explain away as being out of his hands, such that he would only have been involved with them as an unknowing and unwitting participant, "That has always been a question in my mind most of the time, but I'm not gonna sit and lie. I'm not gonna I.D. people, because most of the times [when] I meet women it's in clubs, and in clubs they're supposed to be 21 and over. A lot of times when I meet a woman, it's coming from an after show party. I go to the party and there are all kinds of women there and they're after you, and sometimes I'm after them, too…Being with the wrong crowd or being around a lot of women all the time and that whole thing. The success can get out of hand."

To a degree, Kelly was no different or more at fault than any other young, hot, up-and-coming artist making his bones out on the road early on in a career. Fellow R&B stars like Bobby Brown and Jodeci members KC and JoJo had all developed reputations for being sexually aggressive partiers offstage, a byproduct of the naturally erotic current that ran through their music and lifestyle from the record to the stage and then onto the after parties. As Kelly quickly developed a reputation for antics off-stage that were as wildly erotic as those he displayed on-stage and in song, he clearly sought to be seen as no different from his R&B counterparts. By chalking his rowdy sexual conquests and reputation as a partier and a womanizer up to the inevitable, Kelly argued that his indulgence in the seductive and often morally corrupt elements of success was as natural a part of the process as the making of music itself, "its hard when you're successful to concentrate on anything else but the success—the women, the parties, the clubs, people buying your album, girls screaming your name, and guys going 'woof, woof, woof' before you come out on the stage to perform...It feels good. I'm not going to lie."

Tragically, the runaway success of 12 Play would culminate in heart-break for R. Kelly with the death of his beloved mother, Joanne Kelly, whom he would lose to cancer in late 1993. Growing up as the product of a single-mother household, Kelly, as an adult, even while his mother was still alive in the beginning of his career, sought constantly to identify with the female psyche in song and persona, particularly in the attention he paid to female sensitivities, a center-piece of his lyrical resume, despite being predominantly erotic in message. Many critics and fans alike suspect the latter was in an effort to continually recognize his mother for her role in getting him to the point of manhood where he could mature into the superstar he was fast becoming.

Regardless of his lyrical subject matter, Kelly performed music in large part in celebration of the women in his life, including his mother Joanne, his musical mentor Lena McLin, and his sister, Teresa, all of whom Kelly would write about in the course of his career. It was his mother, above all others, who Kelly sought to acknowledge through song partly in an effort to celebrate her in life and partly in an effort to communicate with her following her tragic demise, "My mama used to always ask me to sing...around the house. She just loved to hear me sing...When I meet people I ask them all the time, 'How close are you to your mother?' That one question will set the tone for my relationship with a person."

Kelly had already endured a lifetime of tragedy by the time of his mother's death and, sadly, he would simultaneously suffer another existence of loss that would haunt him both in song and in spirit. Kelly had measured much of his early success by his mother's ability to share in it, as he explained in an interview following her tragic passing, "With everything that I do, I feel sad...Every day that goes by and another record is sold, I feel sad because I can't call my mother. I loved my mother. I was in love with my mother." Though heartbroken following her death to cancer in 1993, Kelly forged ahead toward the prospect of larger professional successes in the name of his mother's memory, rationalizing that it was what she would have wanted for him, "My mother taught me to fall in love with the future because that way you'll get to the future...She told me not to fall in love with the present because you'll stay in the present or stay in the past. I look to the future every day."

Chapter 4

"Age Ain't Nothing But A Number-
R. Kelly and Aaliyah"

Here I am and there you are
You're eyes are calling me to your hall
All you gotta do is knock and I'll let you in
Then we will feel the passion that flows within
I don't mean to be bold but I gotta let you know
I got a thing for you and I can't let go
—R. Kelly, 'Age Ain't Nothing But a Number'

As late 1993 approached, Tiffany Hawkins, with whom Kelly had engaged in a sexual affair since late 1990, was nearing her 18th birthday. While media speculation has it that, according to Hawkins' civil deposition, intimate relations between the two had cooled some, Kelly was still utilizing both Hawkins and her anonymous Kenwood classmate in the studio and the bedroom. In addition to mentoring the young women in both of the aforementioned locations, Kelly additionally provided them with spending money for things like food and sneakers, possibly in a guilt-based acknowledgment that he had been responsible for their dropping out of high school to work full time for him. This is supported by admissions Kelly made in the course of his 1996 deposition responding to Hawkins' lawsuit wherein he admitted that he employed Hawkins as a background vocalist, and "periodically gave [Hawkins] small cash gifts and…approximately $1,400 in checks." At the time the affair began, while no one can speak with absolute certainty to what was floating around in Kelly's mind, he clearly had something long-term in store with the women. His three-plus years affairs with both women speak in support of his long-term intentions.

While Kelly had taken neither of the girls under his wing as professional protégé's, he had begun to head in that direction with his newest discovery, Aaliyah, and went out of his way, according to Hawkins' classmate and fellow underage Kelly lover, to conduct a more conventional courtship with the 15-year old girl. This meant, for one, keeping Aaliyah away and unaware of the group orgies he is alleged to have regularly indulged in with underage women in his studio and home. Further, Kelly's trysts with such underage partners is said to have continued while he was involved with Aaliyah. While neither allegations have been confirmed, their vulnerability to speculation is less suspect as many women, including Hawkins' anonymous friend, have gone on record to point out that Kelly went out of his way to keep the two parts of his life personally separate. Still, as she recalls, Kelly never sought to involve Aaliyah in any of his other underage rendezvous, principally because he genuinely loved her and "made her feel like they had a monogamous relationship. I really believe that they loved each other."

R. Kelly's marriage to Aaliyah helps to offer a bit of insight into the loss, and lack of trust in people based on that loss, torturing him from within for years. While the media has jumped all over Kelly's illegal marriage to Aaliyah in August, 1994 when she was 15, as evidence of a continued pattern of behavior involving Kelly and underage girls, there was, in truth, much more to the relationship than just fulfillment of R. Kelly's sexual fetish. While most of his early hits were centered either around explicit or implied sexual innuendo, there was another side to Kelly's music that was constantly exploring the absence of true of love and trust in his life. His collaboration with Aaliyah came as an answer to many of Kelly's questions and prayers. He admitted as much in an interview with John Norris on MTV shortly after the scandal over his home-made porn video broke in the media, refusing to answer any direct questions about his relationship with Aaliyah, but making a point to separate the two as having nothing to do with one another, "[My relationship with Aaliyah] was a whole other situation, a whole other time, it was a whole other thing and I'm sure that people also know that."

While the two both admitted to connecting immediately, both in terms of their artistic and physical chemistry, Kelly at the time of their introduction, had an underlying desire to be close to a woman again. Sadly, despite the triumph of 1992 and his breakout hit with Born Into the 90s, a success that his beloved mother had experienced with him during the early stages of his career, the following year proved to be what Kelly has described as his saddest with her mortal passing due to a losing battle with Cancer. Kelly's focus on women as his principal lyrical subject matter went beyond just the sexual. He also sought out love and companionship in his music and displayed an inherent longing for a maternal comfort that would haunt his music for years to come. In an interview following her death, he admitted that, "The people I trust aren't here, and I don't know anybody's motives anymore."

Kelly's relationship with Aaliyah filled several voids while providing him with a creative outlet that allowed him to emote his loss and longing through music. Principally, by serving as producer and principal composer on Aaliyah's debut LP, Kelly was able to exercise some of his own internal frustration and longing for maternal female companionship by connecting vicariously with the female audience on a level that reached far beyond what Kelly as a male sex symbol was capable of.

It was not a leap for Kelly to try to think inside the mind of a woman as a songwriter, as he had grown up around and preferred the company of women for most of his adolescence, describing his upbringing as one in which he was surrounded by, and thus inspired by "women, mostly—my experience with women and my mother's experience with men. I grew up in a house full of women—aunts... a lot of aunts! I've seen them all go through a lot of things with men." Aaliyah had a natural synergy with her audience that came in part simply from being a woman and, as such, her music would touch her female fans in a different way. As there was a pre-existent connection between women that Kelly could never naturally forge with the conflicting messages that his music communicated, he crafted Aaliyah's LP as a means toward revealing to not only his fans, but potential fans he might draw from Aaliyah's listeners, an end in which "I want people to meet the man behind the music as well as the man in the music."

Whether through creative or natural channels, Aaliyah trusted Kelly almost immediately and recalled, "[When] I met Robert...he came to my house and I sang for him, from there we went into the studio and started working together...It came out of nowhere, yet it felt totally natural. I was tripped out." As the two artists began collaborating, Kelly took on the role of mentor to Aaliyah in the studio, and she took on the role of nurturer to Kelly's lost soul. The two fell quickly in love, and on August 31, 1994, at the Sheraton Gateway Suites in Rosemont, Kelly, then 27, and Aaliyah, 15, were married by the Rev. Nathan J. Edmond of Chicago, according to the marriage certificate they filed with the Cook County Clerk. Aaliyah lied on the marriage application about her age at the time, putting it at 18 rather than 15. When the two returned to Chicago to complete post-production on the LP, it was not too long before rumors within their circle of friends and business associates began to fly exposing the nuptials.

'Age Ain't Nothing But a Number,' a title chosen by Kelly for her album, possibly reflecting a subconscious attempt at a defense on Kelly's part at the fact that his romance with the underage singer was immoral in many circles and illegal in the eyes of the law, was Aaliyah's first forte into the record business. With Kelly as her musical mentor and romantic partner everything seemed to fall into place based on the synergy between the two artists, specifically reflecting itself in the chemistry their music reflected. As Aaliyah recalled the making of the first album, she trusted in Kelly completely, "The work was new to me…I worked very hard to make the album perfect. Since Robert did have the experience, he basically laid out the album and everything, but I do want to write and produce my own stuff down the line." However, before the release of the album, Jive Records' publicity machine had already begun fending off media rumors of the illegal union between Kelly and Aaliyah.

As soon as Aaliyah's family found out about the marriage, they demanded it be quickly annulled, and the fledgling R&B singer conceded under pressure. One of the most pointed questions many had at the time was how Aaliyah's manager could have allowed the marriage to take place between she and Kelly when he knew the difference in years between them and was fully aware of both the potential legal and commercial ramifications. This was an especially touchy point as Kelly and Aaliyah's manager, Barry Hankerton, was also Aaliyah's uncle.

Aaliyah's artistic rearing had always been a family affair. Born Aaliyah Dana Haughton, on January 16, 1979 to Michael and Diane Haughton in Bedford Stuyvesant, Brooklyn, New York, Aaliyah, like most Pop stars, showed off her star potential from a young age. Grandmother Mintis L. Hicks Hankerton, would testify to this years later, remarking figuratively that Aaliyah was born "with a full set of hair." At the age of five, Aaliyah and older brother Rashad moved with their parents to Detroit to be closer to Aaliyah's extended family, including Uncle Barry Hankerton, who at the time was married to R&B legend Gladys Knight.

Aaliyah's mother, Diane, doted on her children so much that she left her profession of school teaching to be a stay-at-home mother to Aaliyah and her brother. Like Kelly, Aaliyah grew up in a musical household, raised on the classics of Marvin Gaye and Stevie Wonder. Aaliyah displayed her musical talent at the young age of 5 by memorizing the lyrics to Gaye and Wonder's classics and singing them to her parents and brother around the house.

Recognizing their daughter's talent for music, Aaliyah's parents enrolled her, at the age of 6, in a private Catholic school, Gesu Elementary, in Detroit. This decision was largely based around the school's reputation for outstanding musical productions. Aaliyah's first role as an orphan child in the school's production of Annie was credited with convincing the future R&B star that she desired to be an artist. Local and regional performing in and around the Detroit area paid off at just 11 years old when Aaliyah landed a coveted spot on the nationally syndicated talent show Star Search where she performed "My Funny Valentine" in tribute to her mother. Though she lost the contest, she had caught the ear of her mother's brother, Uncle Barry Hankerton, a record executive who took the young performer under his wing and began her flight toward stardom. At the time, Hankerton was married to Gladys Knight, who played a small, but pivotal, role in encouraging Aaliyah's growth as a performer. Her uncle/manager took Aaliyah at age 11 to Las Vegas to watch and learn from his then-wife, Knight, who was performing a series of five sold-out solo concert dates at Bally's Las Vegas Casino.

Rather than learn from the sidelines, Knight brought Aaliyah on stage where the two dazzled the crowd with a duet of Believe in Yourself. In the course of the same series of performances, Aaliyah dazzled Knight's audience by belting out the solo number "Home." Aaliyah reported years after the experience that the most valuable lesson she left with was fundamentals on how to perform before a crowd. It was Kelly who would later nurture Aaliyah along as a songwriter and artist in the studio, but before Hankerton introduced the two, he signed Aaliyah to his management/production firm, Blackground Enterprises, at the tender age of 13. Thereafter, Aaliyah's career remained a family affair as her mother, Diane Haughton, went on to act as her personal manager; her older brother, Rashad, as creative consultant; her cousin, Jomo Haughton, served as executive producer on later albums; and in addition to continuing to act as her business manager, Uncle Barry Hankerton assumed the role of CEO of her label, Blackground Records, distributed through Jive Records.

Two years later, at age 15, following the writing and recording of Aaliyah's debut LP, Age Ain't Nothing But A Number, Aaliyah was clearly still coming into her own as an artist and still developing an awareness of her own boundless talent, recalling that "as that first album was coming to a finish, I was listening back to the tracks thinking, 'Wow, that's really me. This is how I am and how I sound'...I remember how nervous I was right before 'Back & Forth' came out. It was my first single and I kept wondering if people would accept it. When it went gold, I had my answer and it was such an incredibly satisfying feeling."

The success of the album's first single, "Back and Forth," would be an ironic one in that when it landed atop the Hot 100 singles chart, it knocked her mentor's number one hit at the time, "Your Body's Callin," to number two. As the album introduced and then steadily expanded Aaliyah as a Pop sensation to the teenage masses, light was continually made in the music media of her marriage to Kelly, which, by this point, had been quietly annulled. Still, as both Pop stars continually denied to the public that the union had ever taken place, *Vibe Magazine* settled the issue once and for all by publishing the couple's Michigan marriage license in late 1994. Still, the public knowledge of the marriage had little affect on the momentum of either star's careers as Aaliyah's debut ended the year by going platinum and producing two gold singles: "Back & Forth" and "At Your Best (You Are Love)."

As the album's success took Aaliyah's career off in its own direction, she found herself breaking free of Kelly's wing in the coming years and like many young relationships, theirs, too, came to an end. A fundamental key of Aaliyah's growth beyond Kelly's influence was a natural drive and desire to make her own creative decisions in the studio, in front of the cameras, and on stage. That strive for independence granted her just that from Kelly, though the two remained friends for years to come. As Uncle and manager Barry Hankerton remembers, "[From] the very beginning, [Aaliyah] had a way that she wanted to sound and a way that she wanted to look and she stayed with it. She would be very adamant about those types of creative decisions in her very young career."

Even as Aaliyah moved on in her professional life, she never lost sight of Kelly's influence, but did manage to put it to professional rest as she looked to the future. In looking back, Aaliyah would later recall her debut LP as the foundation that launched her, but would never lose sight of what she felt she was capable of in her own right in future work, "I don't think about my previous success. I'm happy that the work I've done in the past has been very successful. All I can do is leave it in God's hands and hope that my fans feel where I'm coming from. I took the time out to give my all."

For Kelly, the relationship was not a mistake as many in the media would later label it, but rather a cherished time in his life that he continued to treasure and protect from public scrutiny for years after it ended, even in the wake of the Pop singer's tragic death in a plane accident in 2001 and the revived attention his own troubles would bring to the union. In the end, it was obvious that Kelly was not just seeking to protect Aailyah's memory, but also his own memories of their time together, as one of the first times since his mother's passing that he was able to share in true love with a woman, "Aaliyah is gone now, and out of respect for her and her family, I will not discuss [my relationship with] Aaliyah."

As a closing footnote to the couple's relationship, Aaliyah officially closed the book on she and Kelly's union in May, 1997 when she petitioned the court to have the records of the wedding expunged. Kelly's publicist, in the marriage's aftermath, has chosen to characterize Kelly's perspective on the union as something of an acknowledgment that it was a mistake, at the very least, in that both were too young, especially Aaliyah, "[the marriage] ended with, 'Maybe we're over our heads, maybe this is too much, maybe we need to go our separate ways. I love you, I always will, I wish you the best, but maybe we just jumped in way too deep into this thing.' And she went her way and he went his." If only all of Kelly's troubles with underage women could have ended so simply.

Chapter 5

"I Believe I Can Fly"

As R. Kelly's career matured into the mid-1990s, his music began to take on a more serious tone, reflecting what appeared to many to be a personal period of discovery in his life centering around a search for faith. More importantly, Kelly was in the same time struggling to shake a lifestyle that, up to that point, had focused on indulgence. Wherein Kelly's excesses had clearly begun to catch up with his conscience and deeper belief in judgment day, "The bump-and-grind period of my life was just a mood...I've been through a lot in the past two years and I've learned a lot about myself. You can't stay stuck in one groove." He had utilized his gift thus far largely to observe the pompous side of his extremely sexual ego and he now sought to focus on his more pious side in hopes of evolving into a more spiritually-centered performer and individual, "I have to step back and look at this thing like it sho'nuff is...With the gospel, I'm not just trying to entertain. At my age, I'm going through things within myself; thinking about what I want to do in the future; what I'm doing in my life and in my career. I look at whatever I'm doing onstage as taking a step more toward God, because if it weren't for him, I wouldn't be here. The more I live, I'm starting to realize that more and more every day."

While Kelly was clearly looking ahead, it was his mother's passing that had caused him to first begin looking back in deep examination on the first few years of his career. Perhaps questioning his own spiritual conviction in the course of processing his mother's demise or possibly in an effort to more precisely define his professional persona toward his personal goals beyond that of the erotic, Kelly was clearly seeking to grow closer to God, "When my mother passed, she went to Heaven. I truly believe that…The only way I'm going to see her again is if I make it to heaven." Kelly's belief in God had always been peripherally evident in his music, but his lyrical preoccupation with sex had left many critics and fans alike considering him something of a musical contradiction, questioning how connected Kelly truly was to any genuine personal spirituality.

With the release of a new album in November, 1995, simply titled R. Kelly, the singer was clearly looking to make a change in the way his musical direction was heading commercially, seeking to head away from the horny and more toward the holy. One revealing song among the album's collection of more mature tracks was an ode to Kelly's mother, in which Kelly pleads, "Heaven, if you hear me, I need you, Please come back home." It has been widely believed by both fans and critics alike that the term Heaven in the song was code for Mother. More important to Kelly's overall personal direction via the song was his collaboration with gospel star Kirk Franklin, who arranged the ode, and played an important role as spiritual catalyst for Kelly in the early part of 1995 as he sought a more blessed direction in both his professional and personal life. As Franklin first recalled Kelly's reaching out to him, "The brother really motivated me. He called me a few months ago and said, 'Kirk, you know I'm sick and tired of being sick and tired.'"

By linking up with Franklin, Kelly was in effect acknowledging both to himself and to the public that he had grown tired of the way he had been leading his life, clearly acknowledging that he was concerned with the type of behavior he had been engaging in through the course of living the life of a young, charismatic superstar. Before announcing his desire to change to the world, according to *Vibe*

Magazine, he told it quietly to friend, fellow R&B star, and spiritual mentor Kirk Franklin in early 1995, remarking that, "I really want to get some things in my life right with the Lord." Franklin's early attempts to wrestle Kelly away from the perilous lifestyle that had engulfed him up to that point gave what is arguably the best glimpse into Kelly's leading paradox at the time he sought out help.

The crux of this conversation was a struggle to manage his incredible talent alongside the wild lifestyle that routinely competed with it for Kelly's attention, such that, while Franklin readily recognized Kelly's ability, he also easily identified those areas of Kelly's life which were adversely influencing him away from a holier path at the time, "We flew to Chicago to record Rob Kelly…and we flew into Chicago and got in around 6 in the evening, but we didn't record him until 6 in the morning. It was like mad crazy. To wake up at 6 and go, 'OK, [R. Kelly is] ready for everybody to pack up and go to the studio.' His breath was stinkin' [from partying all night before], he had the eye boogers and all that. But it was a blessing. The man is truly gifted from heaven."

Commercially, R. Kelly would be another hit, both validating and confusing Kelly's spiritual search, as the album was quickly certified double platinum by January, 1996, and its first single, "You Remind Me Of Something," was certified platinum. In February, Kelly was nominated for a Grammy Award for Songwriter of the Year for his collaboration with Michael Jackson on "You Are Not Alone," and in March released his second platinum single off of R. Kelly, entitled "Down Low (Nobody Has to Know)," which peaked at the top of the Billboard Hot R&B Singles chart for 7 weeks, the Hot R&B Singles Sales chart for 7 weeks, the Hot R&B Singles Airplay chart for a week, and the Dance Music Maxi-Singles Sales chart for 3 weeks. In June, 12 Play was certified quadruple platinum and R. Kelly triple platinum, as his third album single, "I Can't Sleep Baby (If I)" was released, topping the Billboard R&B Singles Chart for two weeks, and certified immediately platinum in August, 1996.

Though Kelly felt seriously out of touch with God at the time he sought out help, he had been raised in a religious household, crediting his mother for instilling his religious roots, explaining her philosophy as one in which you "put God first, and if you go to do something, you might as well master it." What appeared to be fundamental in Kelly's personal struggle was reconciling a relationship with the Lord that existed in the present and in person, rather than it had in the past very much vicariously through his mother. Kelly had up to the point of her death, seemed to identify with God very much via her as a channel of sorts, where, in her absence, he had no personal understanding of God as an active presence in his life.

For Kelly, the two—God and his mother—were inextricably linked to one another, and his principle challenge lied in separating the two, which presented itself as an especially painful challenge for Kelly given that his principal means of communication and understanding of the presence of God in life had just been delivered to heaven, and out of his world, "When you're successful, especially if you went into it without really having God or church in your life, its hard." Admirably, where others might have become angry or embittered, Kelly sought a higher path that he hoped would ultimately lead him closer to God and to his beloved mother, "When my mother died, I felt that I didn't have anyone to call on anymore. My mom was like God to me because she was a good listener. But not I've started explaining my situation to God. I start every day by praying."

Clearly, in seeking to be born again, Kelly desired, above all else, to have an active relationship with the Lord that he had not had in previous years, such that, despite what fans might think "people will put down and say what they want. It makes me no difference because people are not my God…I don't worry about what people say. That's the point of having a God and knowing who God is, so that you don't have to worry. You give it to God. I believe in myself and in what God has done for me." Defending his religious conversion to the public, specifically to fans who hadn't yet gotten enough of the raunchy, seductive persona that Kelly played out on record, stage, and in video, he rationalized that his personal identity was very much a different thing from his public one, such that "There's R. Kelly and then there's Robert...R. Kelly is a thing on TV, but nobody knows Robert and what he's been through."

In further seeking to relate to fans so that they, too, might embrace his new struggle and sound (and continue to buy his records), Kelly elaborated on his transition, explaining that, "I've been through a lot since my first album. I know I had a lot to say...In the growing of your success, the more you grow. The more you go through... The more you have to write about. It's a big wind. It's like a hurricane sometimes. The more it twists, the more it grows. The more it tears up, the more it spreads. That's pretty much what we're dealing with." Kelly had always acknowledged a divine inspiration as being largely responsible for his seemingly endless talent, remarking to one journalist, "I respect the gift that God has given me as far as music goes." Now, he undoubtedly sought to live God's inspiration in his music rather than merely create music as a result of it. To that end, his first step was to make God a ready priority in both his personal and professional life, such that "what I've physically learned is to put God first in whatever it is I want to accomplish in this music business. Everybody else just isn't Him."

Kelly began on this path, musically at least, by refocusing his musical message to fans explaining that through his songs, he desired his listeners to "feel motivated. I want them to feel they can touch the sky, leap over the moon. I want them to feel that they can accomplish their goals." In changing his musical direction, Kelly was almost identically altering his personal direction, and in unison, the two began on a journey toward spiritual enlightenment that, Kelly told one journalist at the time, began with both acknowledgment and concession, by saying, "[I just began to believe that there was] something bigger and better out there...For the most part, all I was doing was feeding my body, doing what made me feel good."

Acknowledging that he had been selfishly focused with much of his early songwriting was something of a first step toward absolution from what he viewed as sins of the past. Kelly revealed at the time, "I'm at the point now where I'm saying, 'I know I got famous from doing these sex songs, but I know there is a God; I believe there is a God.'"

The next step in Kelly's conversion involved refocusing the direction of his music, where, as spiritual advisor Kirk Franklin looked at it, "Robert doesn't have to do a gospel album to please God. But his subject will have to grow. His dialogue is gonna have to change. God can give him songs to do about real relationships. Why does every song have to be Stick it, lick it, screw it?" In shedding much of his superficial skin, Kelly was able to begin the process of getting to know a side of himself that appeared up unto that point to have been largely alien to him. As his conversion process got underway, he was engaging in a period of intense self-reflection, remarking at one Franklin concert several months after his initial realization that "its been a long time coming, but here I am…It amazes me when I look back eight months ago—cars, women, money, the media. I had everyone's attention [but the Lords']…Every day I seem to be falling in love with the Lord." In a very real way, Kelly seemed ashamed of the life he had been leading, remarking that before a crowd of thousands "here [before you] stands a broken man…Some may think it's a gimmick, but I tell you…I've come to find out that whatever you want, its in the Lord."

In the course of his religious conversion, Kelly began his real trial with the recording of his third album, R. Kelly, which reflected, in many ways a complete 180-degree turn from the erotic nature of the music Kelly had made his name on up to that point. With titles such as "The Sermon," "Heaven If You Hear Me," "Religious Love," and perhaps the album's most revealing song, "Trade in My Life," which Kelly recorded with Franklin and which Kelly dedicated to his deceased mother. While Kelly was eager to head out commercially with the results of his personal enlightenment and recommitment to God, he clearly felt nervousness on some level concerning how fans would receive his new sound, so much that in one interview after another surrounding the album's release in the summer of 1995, Kelly sought to paint his music's renewed spiritual focus as a natural step in his larger career direction, rationalizing that "sex doesn't control me. Take away the sexy bump and grind, and you can easily put in the gospel lyrics."

With the release of R. Kelly, Jive Records geared up for what they hoped would be a platinum reception to Kelly's refocused musical message with the label's Senior Marketing Director Jazzy Jordan remarking at the time that "a lot of people will be surprised by Robert's level of sophistication on this album...Its going to open for him in other areas. He's one of the few true performers in R&B today that can move as easily in one direction as the next." In attempting to be truly clued in and respectful of Kelly's altered musical direction, the label chose a more spiritual song, "You Remind Me of Something" as the album's first single, with Jordan explaining, "We didn't want to be so [commercially] obvious and release ["Be Happy"] first. We feel "You Remind Me of Something" is more representative of where Robert is going with his music and will reach a broader audience."

While the release of 1995's R. Kelly reflected something of a musical rebirth for Kelly in the more mature focus of the album's songs, he clearly felt he was still far from being ready to record an album focused entirely on God in theme, i.e. a full-on Gospel album, "[Someday] I believe I will. Sometimes I believe I will end up singing Gospel [exclusively]...But I can't sing Gospel unless I'm all the way with the Lord. Its like a school thing. Its like when you start off with school, you can't start off graduating. You can't start off knowing. There are questions that have to be asked, and there are questions that have to be answered...That is my desire to one day be with God and the whole thing. But its all about being real with myself. I believe, eventually, people are going to hear a Gospel album, but I believe its going to be real. I believe once it does happen for me in that area of my life, then I'm going to be completely that. I don't want to be in/out, in/out, in/out. That's my wish."

In addition to his feeling personally uncommitted to an entirely Gospel-themed album, Kelly felt any attempt that wasn't completely reflective of personal conviction and religious commitment would be inappropriately received by fans and ultimately would be sac-religious in what Kelly viewed as a very significant personal journey he was on toward oneness with the Lord, "I would be setting me up, my fans up, and lying to God...You have to be grounded and groomed for something as big as that. You have to take it a step at a time."

Still, despite Kelly's self-doubts about his abilities to reach the spiritual heights than he felt a true Gospel album would require to accomplish, others within the recording industry, including critic Nelson George expressed confidence that Kelly, as the decade's most gifted R&B talent, would be up to task, and that all would be watching in similar belief and expectation, "I don't know what triggered R. Kelly to say the things that he did [toward spiritual revival], whether it was one particular event like it was for Al Green who said God spoke to him one morning, or whether it was many things. But whatever it was, his decision will be watched closely...He could do both Gospel and R&B or he could simply write love songs with less explicit language. It wouldn't be suicidal to his career unless he gets really negative and renounces everything he's done [up to this point]. It's a matter of degree."

Following the release of his third album in 1995, an extremely trying and intense period of spiritual discovery whose greatest single challenge Kelly had summarized as, "Being consistent about being consistent," the superstar was approaching what many critics believed to be a point of legitimate musical enlightenment that could only have been religiously inspired late in the year, when, at the request of friend and Chicago Bulls superstar Michael Jordan,

Kelly penned what would become his biggest and most inspired hit, "I Believe I Can Fly." "I Believe I Can Fly" was Kelly's first real attempt to let the world know he had reached a personal level of higher spiritual enlightenment, such that Kelly believed the song was truly a result of the touch of God where he came to "believe that God wrote that song because it was so special when it came to me...It was not like any of the other songs I've written. I was going through a lot of things when this song came to me. It was really ministering to me. It made me feel good and gave me life. It made me feel that anybody...It was more powerful than anything I've ever had to do with. That's why I feel like I didn't have anything to do with it..."I Believe I Can Fly" [is] something else, that's a whole other level...I was just the one used for that particular song to come out for my own self and for others as well."

Quick to become a favorite of church choirs nationwide, the song was the best evidence yet that Kelly had made progress in his journey, growing as both a person and a songwriter by broadening both his awareness of the Lord and his ability to reach and affect a larger listening audience through that divine consciousness. Kelly elaborated at the time of the song's release on the latter, explaining that his songwriting had grown beyond its early focus on the bedroom in an effort to "reach out and touch other people...As a songwriter, I [now] write from feelings and experiences. Some songs are based on passion, which is something I think we all feel deep inside. Some songs are more emotional—like a cry out to the world."

The song's release was a testing ground for Kelly, and the reaction it received from fans worldwide was a genuine acknowledgment that he was on the right path. Commercially, the song performed heavenly, topping the Billboard Hot 100 Singles Sales chart for 7 weeks, the Hot R&B Singles chart for 6 weeks, the Hot R&B Singles Sales chart for 5 weeks, and the Hot R&B Singles Airplay chart for 2 weeks, and ultimately won him a Grammy Award.

Kelly's shift in focus to the spiritual over the sexual brought with it the doors to the Pop music kingdom, allowing Kelly the opportunity to expand and upgrade his collaborative resume in late 1995 and early 1996 to include collaborations with the créme of Pop's crop, including its reigning king, Michael Jackson, for whom Kelly composed and produced the chart-topper "You Are Not Alone." In writing for Michael Jackson, Kelly approached the experience with a mix of confidence and childlike nervousness at the opportunity to work with one of his childhood idols. As Kelly explained at the time, "I was psyched…I feel I could have done his whole album. Not being selfish. I was just that geeked about it. It was an experience out of this world…Its amazing to know that five years ago I was writing songs in a basement in the ghetto and now I'm writing for Michael Jackson…[who] came to Chicago to work with me…I'd be a fool not to say it's a dream come true."

Kelly clearly felt that the bigger the opportunity, the better he would perform, and in that spirit, broadcast to all listening ears that "whoever reaches out to me, I'm going to give them my best…It makes me feel good to take someone from one level and take them higher, whether they're known or whether they've never been known. That's my job, that's what I do, and that's what I love. I have a passion for that—not just writing songs, but taking people to certain levels." Addressing concerns that his penchant for self-promotion might be getting ahead of his ability to deliver in the studio, Kelly qualified his confidence by citing the circumstances under which he had come to work with Jackson, explaining, "He reached out to me and asked if I had anything laying around. I was amazed when he called me, because I just didn't expect to go to that level. It was an honor to work with him…When he got the tape, he called me backstage at a show and said 'When can we cut this?' It was truly a blessing…It was a very big honor…It wasn't exactly another day in the office for me…We spent days together working in the studio, we got to know each other and how each other works and respect the art. I had to argue with him on that song! Make him sing it! He wanted the K-Ci & JoJo track ["Life," the title track from the Eddie Murphy motion picture soundtrack]. I told him, 'This song is you, trust me. It's gonna be big…' He settled down and got into it."

In elaborating on the nuts and bolts of his work in the studio with Jackson, Kelly revealed a bit about his mental process in preparing to write for artists outside of his immediate genre namely by establishing a creative cohesion by copycatting their style to make it temporarily his own, to the point where "when I'm in [the studio] doing a Michael Jackson song, I think I am him. I become him. I want him to feel that too. That's why I record the vocals sounding just like him. When I gave him "You Are Not Alone" and he heard me doing his runs, he laughed. But I wanted him to feel how much I was feeling him." Kelly's collaboration with Pop Diva Celine Dion pushed him further into the mainstream as both a songwriter and performer, allowing even further declassification of his talent as limited strictly to R&B or Pop-crossover from that vein alone, a process Kelly described as simply about the music, "When I wrote "I'm Your Angel," I said to myself, 'Man, this reminds me of Celine Dion.' I said, 'I'm gonna call her and see if she would be interested in doing this with me.' I felt the song needed a female voice, and that's who I heard… I called and she accepted; I was honored. The thing I love about her most is that it wasn't about color, it wasn't about who's who and what's what, it wasn't about R&B or Pop, it was about a song that meant something to her, to me. It had no color." Additional collaborations during this period for Kelly included his penning and/or producing songs for the likes of Janet Jackson, Toni Braxton, Quincy Jones, Whitney Houston, and the Isley Brothers.

The commercial success of the collaboration, for Kelly, went beyond the immediate hit in further broadening industry acceptance of his talent, allowing its transcendence beyond the traditional R&B and even Pop quarters, and into genres that had historically been off-limits to writers and performers Popular in Kelly's R&B/Soul medium. Kelly clearly viewed himself as an equal, which allowed him to dare his next collaboration with the king of Country music, pushing him to what could have been an almost paradoxical point had it not been for Kelly's chameleon-like talent as he reasoned by saying, "[Putting] together a song for [country singer] Garth Brooks…I don't like to think of myself as an R&B artist [any-more]…I've been through too much, been to too many places; writ-ten songs from Country to Pop, Blues to Jazz to Gospel… I can't label myself as 'an R&B artist.' When you've done what I've done, been where I've been, it's kinda hard to label yourself as one thing."

Kelly's larger goal with his songwriting appeared to be for its eventual freedom from labels as he felt God had brought him to a point where he could travel above and beyond any boundaries that musically encompassed peers of lesser holy conviction by saying that "I wish that what they call Pop, what they call R&B, and Soul were all just one thing, because I will write anything. I don't really get into a cer-tain category when I'm writing. The gospel feel is always mixed up in there because I grew up that way—I came out of the church. But whatever comes to my heart and my ears and I hear, I will write it."

As Kelly began to settle down musically in late 1995 and early 1996, he also sought to do so personally. To that end, Kelly began to attempt an end too much of his underage sexual trysts, severing relations with Tiffany Hawkins, then 18, and focusing on creating an ideal homestead. Kelly had attained the wealth necessary to secure the life for a family that he as a child had never had, going as far as creating bedrooms for offspring he had yet to conceive in his newly-purchased and renovated suburban Chicago mansion, which a journalist for *Ebony Magazine* described as "the centerpiece of Kelly's home…Although he says he doesn't have children [yet]… Kelly says he likes to spend time in [the kids'] room, which is fur-nished with television sets and a wall mural of him interacting with several cartoon characters."

In describing the rest of Kelly's dream home, a true reflection of his dreams attained and indulged, the journalist painted the portrait of "a breathtaking mansion on Chicago's exclusive Near North side. Converted from a church, the multi-million dollar home was painstakingly renovated last year by one of the city's top architectural firms, Restrepo Group Inc. The home, in which [Kelly] lives about one week out of every month, has an indoor basketball court [with its own sound system], an indoor pool, a dance studio, and a 1,500-gallon shark-filled aquarium that is built into the wall. The wall aquarium, an idea Kelly got from a James Bond movie, also was home to several stingrays, until they were eaten by the sharks... The great room includes a wall-hugging stairway that rises 27 feet and overlooks a grand piano, home-theatre system, and marble chess board, which is embedded in the floor."

Kelly personally explained away the extravagances of the home as a matter of practicality, reasoning, "When I'm not on the road, I'm at home most of the time." Another of Kelly's rewards to himself for several years of endless touring and recording was a state-of-the-art recording studio he had constructed at the time, which he described as something that wasn't "going to be some big art gallery or anything like that. I'm building it where light makes things happen. Light is very important to me. A lot of times I write a song with a shade of light showing through the window with no lights on inside; just natural light...It reminds me of the days when my grandmother fixed me oatmeal. The light would shine through the window at 8 o'clock in the morning. That's a very important thing in the way I'm building the studio. Its not going to be that big, but it will do the job."

In attempting to reel his wild ways toward a more refined and long-term definition of what he desired in a companion, much of what he sought was clearly derivative of what he loved in his own mother, so much that as Kelly described his ideal women to one journalist, he explained that "there's a bone-deep sensuality that I love about black women. For example, whenever my mother and I talked over tea, I remember how she would leave her lipstick print on the teacup. Seeing that moved me for reasons I'm not even sure I understand. So when I'm out with a young lady, chillin' and drinking tea, if she's wearing lipstick and leaves her print on the cup, I find myself falling in love with her—at least for that moment. Love is real for me when that one special lady not only gets inside my head and really understands me, but also makes me believe I can do anything. My mom, who passed away last year, was special like that. She set the tone for my involvement with the ladies. So when I find a woman who makes me feel like I can knock down Chicago's Sears Tower, all I can say is. 'That's it!'"

Kelly found that woman in late 1996 when he married a 22-year-old dancer from his touring troupe who would later give birth to his two daughters, fulfilling his dream of a family of his own. Kelly's decision to settle down and begin a family was part of a larger effort to put his partying past behind him, though the singer, himself, would admit at the time that that effort was an ongoing and extremely challenging one, "I'm growing and it's a part of growing. You start seeing yourself for who you really are because you start seeing life for what it really is and you start having kids and a family and a wife and stuff. You don't want to hurt the ones you love and you don't want to make the same mistakes." Though Kelly had made great strides between late 1994 and early 1996 to put the past behind him, it would catch up with him, unfortunately, before he would get the opportunity to shake it, and Kelly once again would seek, through out-of-court settlements with several woman who sued him beginning in 1996 alleging, among other charges, that he engaged with them in sexual relationships while they were still underage, to hide a truth that ultimately would reveal itself to the world in the years to come and threaten to ruin everything Kelly had worked to build for himself in the course of his spiritual reconstruction.

Photo Gallery

R. Kelly (2nd right) poses with his first group M.G.M. back in the day, on the set of their video for their debut single, "Why You Wanna Play Me" ('89)

photo by Raymond Boyd

After his group M.G.M. disbanded, R. Kelly (pointing) formed Public Announcement. Here, they pose moments before taking the stage at the Regal Theater in Chicago. ('92)   photo by Raymond Boyd

R. Kelly performs during an in-store appearance for the release of his CD 12 Play at George's Music Room in Chicago. (Dec. '93)

photo by Raymond Boyd

At a party in his honor, R. Kelly poses with his platinum plaque for his CD 12 PLAY and the single, SEX ME (Parts I & II). (Dec. '93)

photo by Raymond Boyd

R. Kelly meets up with comedian George Wallace at his platinum party in Chicago. (Dec. '93)   *photo by Raymond Boyd*

R. Kelly and his dancers perform during the video for his single, "Bump 'n' Grind" at the Vic Theater in Chicago. ('94)

photo by Raymond Boyd

At his multi-platinum party at Inta's in Chicago, R. Kelly and comedian Bernie Mac share a photo. (April '94)   photo by Raymond Boyd

R. Kelly greets well-wishers at a party in his honor at Inta's in Chicago. (April '94)
photo by Raymond Boyd

R. Kelly, in concert during his "12 Play Tour" at Chicago's U.I.C. Pavilion.
(May '94)   *photo by Raymond Boyd*

R. Kelly performs at the WGCI-FM Music Seminar at the Hyatt Hotel in Chicago (June '94)   *photo by Raymond Boyd*

R. Kelly poses during his in-store appearance for his CD, R. Kelly at George's Music Room in Chicago. (Nov. '95)

photo by Raymond Boyd

R. Kelly spends a private moment with his dog "12 Play" during a break in rehearsals for his "Down Low Tour" in Los Angeles. (March '96)
photo by Raymond Boyd

R. Kelly and his younger brother Carey pose together on the set of Kelly's video for "Thank God It's Friday" in Los Angeles. (March '96)

Photo by Raymond Boyd

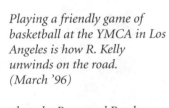

Playing a friendly game of basketball at the YMCA in Los Angeles is how R. Kelly unwinds on the road. (March '96)

photo by Raymond Boyd

Before going to the studio to rehearse in Los Angeles, R. Kelly finds himself having a bowl of "Cap 'N Crunch Peanut Butter Crunch" cereal in his hotel room. (March '96)   *photo by Raymond Boyd*

In the studio is where R. Kelly does his magic. That was no different in this Los Angeles studio where Kelly puts the magic down for his "Down Low Tour". (March '96)   *photo by Raymond Boyd*

*R. Kelly tries on some outfits in
his room for consideration for
his "Down Low Tour" while
rehearsing in Los Angeles
(March '96)*

photos by Raymond Boyd

R. Kelly poses for a photo after a press conference in Chicago announcing his I Believe I Can Fly celebrity basketball game. (Aug. '97)

photo by Raymond Boyd

R. Kelly greets singer Brian McKnight, who announced his participation in R. Kelly's celebrity basketball game in Chicago.

photo by Raymond Boyd

R. Kelly shoots a free throw during his 1st Annual I Believe I Can Fly celebrity basketball game in Chicago.

photo by Raymond Boyd

R. Kelly was the keynote speaker during the WGCI-FM Music Seminar in Chicago. (May '98)

photo by Raymond Boyd

R. Kelly in concert at the WGCI-FM "Big Jam" concert at the United Center in Chicago. (May '99)

photos by Raymond Boyd

A bearded R. Kelly poses for photographers while attending "R. Kelly Day" at Chicago's "Expo for Today's Black Woman". (Apr. '00)

photo by Raymond Boyd

R. Kelly poses on the set of his video, The World's Greatest in Chicago. (Oct. '01)

photo by Raymond Boyd

R. Kelly takes a playful jab at video director Billie Woodruff during a break in filming Kelly's video, The World's Greatest in Chicago (Oct. '01)

photo by Raymond Boyd

R. Kelly films his video The World's Greatest for the "Ali" movie soundtrack in Chicago (Oct. '01)   photo by Raymond Boyd

R. Kelly performs during the WGCI-FM "Big Jam II" concert at the United Center in Chicago. (Dec. '01)

photo by Raymond Boyd

R. Kelly on Tour

Photos on next three pages by Walik Goshorn

*R. Kelly meets with the press at George's Music Room in Chicago to discuss his new CD **Chocolate Factory** (March '03)*

photo by Raymond Boyd

R. Kelly greets a fan during his in-store autograph signing at George's Music Room in Chicago (March '03) photo by Raymond Boyd

Chapter 6

"Falling Apart at the Seams"

"I've known Robert for many years, and I've tried to get him help," says one person who split from the inner circle over the issue. "Robert's problem is little girls."

—*Spin Magazine*

R. Kelly's break-up with Aaliyah in late 1994 put him back in a dangerous place with his personal insecurities concerning trust, and as his career continued to sky-rocket, Kelly was again looking for love and acceptance in all the wrong places. He admitted in an interview where he conceded that by indulging the attention of the fans and groupies who admired him for his talents, he opened himself up to be taken advantage of in the process, "I'm a real person, and I love people. That's my problem. I let people into my world, and they fuck some things up." It was this period of indulgence and excess that first caused Kelly, in late 1995, to seek out the council and advice of Gospel star Kirk Franklin who, at the time, assisted him toward making serious strides toward reforming what Kelly felt were the out-of-control areas of his personal life. He even inspired the R&B superstar to change musical direction in mid-career—a career feat not easily achieved for any star.

Prince pulled it off in the early 1990s to some degree by changing his name to an unpronounceable symbol in an effort to combat Warner Bros. over contractual differences, but Kelly was not trying to hide from a name, or a past for that matter, he was working hard to put what he acknowledged to be an unnamed problem behind him, which he later openly acknowledged to be "a problem with women...we're all human and I'm dealing with something. And I'm not ashamed to say [it]." Kelly has rooted much of his problem back to the time immediately following his mother's death, particularly his inability to have known who he should have surrounded himself with in the way of advisors, since his mother had been his biggest influence up to that point. Kelly revealed this in an interview with one reporter, where he lamented that "the people I trust aren't here...and I don't know anybody's motives anymore." In light of this, Kelly described his immediate instinct in the wake of her passing as one in which "I didn't want to live anymore...I put a gun to my head and all that." And though Kelly eventually saw the light and put the dark period of insecurity, which led him to use poor judgment, and lack of appropriate discretion in his choice of coping partners, mainly underage women, behind him, that period of his life began to catch up to him through his private life.

On December 24, 1996, Tiffany Hawkins, the woman whom Kelly ended an illicit sexual relationship with upon her turning 18, presented him with a lawsuit loaded with allegations that threatened to blow Kelly's career to pieces. Hawkins' suit, filed in Cook County Circuit Court of Chicago, Illinois, against Kelly personally as well as his label, Jive Records, his publishing company, and management organization. Hawkins charged, among other allegations, that she had been subjected to three years of personal injury and severe emotional damage due to what she alleged to be an intense, three-year sexual relationship with the singer that began when she was 15 and still a student at Kenwood Academy and lasted until late 1994, when she turned 18, during which time she engaged in repeated instances of intercourse with Kelly as well as group sex acts with other underage girls at Kelly's urging. She also charged that Kelly encouraged her to drop out of school and work full-time for him as an employee, which also put Kelly in potential violation of a number of sexual harassment laws.

Kelly counter-sued for $30,000, but eventually made the decision to settle after hearing the contents of a 7-plus hour deposition in 1998, agreeing to a $250,000 settlement with Hawkins out of court in exchange for her sealed testimony—silence. Kelly's label sought to distance themselves from the lawsuit at the time, not by supporting Kelly's content, but rather by arguing in their formal response to the suit that, "[Kelly's] alleged tortuous conduct against his live-in paramour in the privacy of their home has nothing to do with [Jive and Zomba]."

In fleshing out Kelly's M.O., Susan Loggans, an attorney who represented Hawkins as well as several other plaintiffs in suits against Kelly, described a repetitive scenario played out time after time over the years where "Typically, [Kelly] meets girls at parties…Usually, they're South Side girls, and he invites them to his recording studio…[Concerning one alleged victim, according to Loggans], Kelly told her, 'I'll listen to you; maybe I'll use you as a back up singer.' Then he gets involved in a sexual relationship with them." In Hawkins' case, Kelly eventually admitted to having an association with the girl in which the two were acquaintances and that he "periodically gave [her] small cash gifts and…approximately $1,400 in checks." According to the *Chicago Sun-Times*, another woman named in Hawkins' lawsuit as a corroborative witness to the teen's accusations was prepared to testify at the time to what she termed a "sickness" on Kelly's part in regard to his pursuit of underage women. According to the woman, who chose to remain an anonymous source to the story, she alleged to have had sexual relations with Kelly through the year 1991, when she was merely 16, and Kelly had just begun his affair with Hawkins. Her knowledge of Kelly's tryst with the then 15-year-old Hawkins stemmed principally from an alleged encounter wherein she had intercourse with Kelly while he fondled Hawkins. The woman, looking back on the affair, remarked to the journalist in retrospect that she had decided to come forward out of a sense of inevitability, "I just feel like it's going to come out in the light anyway…I'm not trying to [bring him down], because really, honestly, I think it has to be a sickness. Looking at the pictures of how me and Tiffany were when we were freshmen, we were ugly little girls compared to what he could have had, and so I just didn't understand why he did what he did."

What made the woman's corroboration seem most credible, aside from its detail, was the fact that she had no financial motive invested in coming forward. Another friend of Hawkins', though not directly involved in the affair, confirmed her allegations in a cover story for the *Chicago Times* in 2000, remarking to the journalist that "I just don't understand why he did what he did." Many would wonder publicly in later years, but Kelly, for the moment, had staved off his first of what would be many spiders to appear from the woodwork in the years that followed.

In further elaborating on Kelly's pattern of behavior with Hawkins and women like her in the context of his larger off-stage lifestyle, it is crucial to examine Kelly's own mental disposition at the time, specifically those insecurities which led him to surround himself with company regardless of their motives in associating with him and who may not have had his best interests in mind. Kelly characterized this period as centering around "women or partying too much. It's not just women. Of course I have no shame in saying I love women, and I do, and I probably always will, but I have a problem with trusting people, just like I have a problem being around the wrong people…You know, people taking my CDs out of the studio and selling them. There's an album out there right now that they claim is my album and it's all over the place. Somebody got it out of my studio because I got too many people in the studio…The women thing. The so-called friends thing. I probably spend like $2 million a year just on Chinese food and pizza for everybody because I got these 10 people in the studio that don't sing or that don't produce." The invasion by groupies into Kelly's life was not uncommon to any number of high-profile Pop star personalities over time. In part, his tolerance of their overindulgence and penchant for taking advantage of him at a weak point in his life was understandable given his recent loss and lack of direction.

However, Kelly, in the same time, acknowledged being conscious of the abuse by his entourage of groupies and tolerating it no matter how far over the line they went. He felt that because he was in need of companions, no matter their caliber of character (or lack thereof), he let them pull him down willingly, "Sometimes I get egotistical...Sometimes I'm R. Kelly and I really just wanna be Robert. Sometimes I'm influenced by [the wrong] people. You know what I'm saying? Sometimes I wanna take a drink, sometimes I don't, and sometimes I may do it because somebody says, 'Hey man, let's go drink.'" In further elaborating on his vice, Kelly explained to one journalist during this period that he felt helpless to change until some greater influence came into his life to overpower those that were weakening him "Every night is a low point in my life...And every night will continue to be a low point until I reach a certain point where I learn how to take control of my life and not do certain things anymore." Kelly, in later years, would admit to MTV reporter John Norris that at one point he did, indeed, have a problem with overindulging in women, though not pinning himself down to their specific age group, "As far as women in general, I do honestly believe that your fame has a lot to do with why you get with women. I walk into a club and I can come out with two or three women, and that's a problem for me. I was living the life of R. Kelly."

Beyond the alleged sexual misconduct running rampant through Kelly's life from the early 1990s on through the middle of the decade, even once he had begun to seek out help and turn his life around, Kelly's past would not shake him so easily. Kelly often traveled with a portable basketball court on tour, and would set up in different cities in-between shows to play pick-up games with members of his entourage and different locals. Though he approached the game with extreme professionalism, signing a contract in 1997 with the United States Basketball League's Atlantic City Seagulls as a reserve guard, his pick-up games tended to follow more of a street code of conduct, so much that in 1996, four men filed suit against Kelly and five of his bodyguards alleging they were beaten during a pick-up game during a tour stopover in Lafayette, Louisiana. In early 1997, Kelly was arrested when stopping through the city for another tour date for failure to appear for a deposition hearing relative to the suit. Perhaps he declined to initially respond to the suit out of fear of his possible guilt, or possibly he regarded it as one of many frivolous lawsuits logged against him, and as such, beneath his time or attention.

Eventually, Kelly alleged in his response that the locals had started the brawl with racial slurs following their side's losing the pick-up game. Though the judge eventually dismissed the suit, she implied in her remarks at the time that some of those people who Kelly was still choosing to surround himself with, even following his efforts to reform wayward associations in the recent past through his partnership with Kirk Franklin and recommitment to a holier life, were still the cause of his legal difficulties, implying a continuum in a pattern of behavior Kelly had made significant attempts to shake, "Mr. Kelly, you have been very ill-served by the people who surround you."

By quietly settling the Hawkins suit as his career and personal life continued to blossom toward a brighter future direction in 1997 and into the beginning of 1998, it could be argued that Kelly was remaining consistent in his efforts to make amends with what he viewed as a troubled personal past, possibly stemming from his guilt over engaging in the type of behavior with underage women alleged in Hawkins' lawsuit. However, in hindsight, Kelly, himself, has admitted regret over settling the suits, suggesting that his decision at the time had been misconstrued by the public as an insinuation that he had something larger to hide, whereas if he had opted to fight the suits publicly at the time of their filing, he might have insulated himself from future judgment, and contradicted any assertion that he was not ready to completely own up to that dark part of his past, "I know I got a reputation out there and I really do believe because of the two lawsuits in the past that I settled, I do believe that me being famous has left a trail of people trying to come at me, and then rumor got around also that I settle things. I pay money to make it go away. That's why I really wish I hadn't done that."

In truth however, Kelly had paid money to make the Hawkins' suit go away, and would do so time and again in the last half of the decade, as his alleged past conduct with underage women continued to haunt him. What Kelly's continued pattern of concealment would additionally imply was that despite his best efforts to get beyond any alleged problem with pursuing underage women, if one were to go by the additional lawsuits that were filed against and settled quietly by Kelly into 2001 when rumors of the taped encounter began to surface, it appeared that he was, in fact, still very much in the midst of an active struggle with his demons.

Amid his categorical denials of the larger charge that he had a problem with sexually pursuing underage girls, Kelly seemed in his more intimate and honest interview moments over the course of a period stemming from 1998 through 2002 to acknowledge that there were some darker tendencies that included mainly women and groupies in his life that were not totally part of the past, but, rather, still present in their adverse impact on Kelly's attempts to reconcile with those demons in an effort to become one with the Lord. Furthermore, what appeared to be Kelly's own guilt over their presence in his life seemed to stand in direct contradiction to battling whatever darker side of his personality that continued to invite them in.

Principally, it appeared that despite Kelly's knowledge of the adverse presence of those destructive influences exemplified through his admitted guilt over their continuation in his life, this awareness on Kelly's part was, in and of itself, ultimately not strong enough to inhibit those negative influences from, at times, taking over his judgment or lack thereof, "[I know the negative influences are there and are wrong], but then I turn around and love them anyway, because that's what I want God to do for me...I forgive them...because I want to be forgiven one day." This would continue to be Kelly's struggle for years to come, despite the continuum in his career heights which would ultimately serve to bring a greater breadth of attention to Kelly's alleged problems than he ever would have bargained for.

Chapter 7

"TP-2K"

As the 1990s approached their sunset years of 1998–2000, R. Kelly firmly cemented his place in R&B crossover history. Not only that, but he succeeded any real labeling through his work as a songwriter for artists of every genre. In the years following 1997's Grammy-winning smash "I Believe I Can Fly," R. Kelly had drawn comparisons to Stevie Wonder's "Songs in the Key of Life" with the 1998 release of his fourth album, simply titled R., which debuted in the Billboard top 10 in November, 1998. It consisted of a staggering 30 tracks, garnered critical raves, sold upward of seven million albums, and produced the hit singles "I'm Your Angel" (a duet with Celine Dion), "If I Could Turn Back the Hands of Time," and "When a Woman's Fed Up." In February of 1998, Kelly took home three Grammy awards for Best R&B Song, Best Song Written Specifically for a Motion Picture, and Best Male R&B Vocal Performance, and in March, won the BMI Award for Pop Songwriter of the Year ["I Believe I Can Fly," "I Can't Sleep Baby (If I)," and "I Don't Want To," recorded by Toni Braxton.)

Kelly, eight years into his career, had sold over thirty million albums worldwide, and with the release of R., He was receiving heaps of critical praise for not only the album's sleek production and catchy songwriting, but also for the variety of musical styles it encompassed so much that around the time of the album's release, Kelly was clearly ready for a new level of critical acceptance that he felt should be equal to that of his commercial milestones, "I definitely don't think that [my style of] music gets fair recognition in the mainstream, y'know?…I've never thought that. [My] music doesn't get its fair shake."

Perhaps Kelly's inability to have his commercial cake and eat it too thus far had to do with his music's thematic inconsistence, rooting principally in what many critics panned as Kelly's penchant for wearing too much of his heart on his sleeve, filling his albums with too many conflicting messages to ever achieve one coherent direction for anyone to follow. Kelly defended his right to mix messages and air his dirty laundry on record, namely his personal struggle with sex vs. salvation, arguing that his fans appreciated his attempts to come clean on record with them about everything he was struggling personally within his life largely because many of his listeners were experiencing similar personal dilemmas and because he felt his music was therapeutic for both he and his fans as a result "this is America. I've always said I've got a few issues that I'm dealing with. In my music, I cry. It's a cry. People that listen to me know that. They know my heart is honest about the fact that I'm no angel here. I'm trying to come out. I got songs that are great, beautiful, "I Believe I Can Fly" songs and I got these "Bump N' Grind" songs, but that's a struggle." Despite the fact that he may have still sinned now and then, Kelly made significant personal progress in his quest to become closer to God, explaining that "now, I just have a better vision…a better way of going about being religious."

Whether or not Kelly worked out his personal conflict over the best way to spend his time, i.e. in the bedroom or the church, he seemed professionally to have established a happy personal medium between the two essentially by splitting the lyrical content of his albums down the middle. While he had already made his mark in early days with sexually explicit titles like "I like the Crotch on You," "You Remind Me of Something," and the seminal "Bump N' Grind," in the mid-1990s, Kelly made a notable switch to a more holy musical direction, penning such titles as "The Sermon" and "Heaven If You Hear Me," and by the time the release of 1998's R. rolled around, the singer seemed content with trying to juggle both, arguing to one journalist that it was ok for him to continue to produce sexually-suggestive music, reasoning that "there's nothing wrong with a little bumping and grinding. None of us would be here if it wasn't for that."

Still, Kelly's commercial successes beyond his R&B audience had put him on a larger, more global stage, with bigger critics to answer to and more potential fan bases to tap into for expanded record sales.

Toward that end, Kelly embraced a more mature commercial direction with the marketing of his newest album, explaining his departure from music purely sexual or religious in topic as a reflection of his own personal growth as both a person and an artist, "At first that's going to be a bit exciting, a bit out of control. But if you live long enough, God will bless you long enough to realize that it ain't just about that. It's about maintaining your success because if you keep going that route, you're going to drain yourself." Kelly further sought to flesh out for listening ears and reading eyes at the time what the very soul of his songwriting was trying to say to the world, specifically his female audience, beyond just his sexual lamentations.

Kelly felt he had grown greatly as a songwriter over the years and, specifically on his latest album, not just in his ability to write in the shoes of other artists, but also in those of his female fans, to the point where he could relate directly to them on a human level as well, "When it comes to the relationship songs, I'm more, like, being apologetic—'I'm sorry. I should have been more man about it. I should have listened to you' or 'This time I decided I'm gonna stay home tonight. I ain't goin' nowhere. I'm dumping my friends and staying with you,' situations like that."

More importantly, Kelly viewed his growth as a songwriter as a reflection of personal maturity, specifically toward the women in his own life, such that, as Kelly reasoned, the two went hand in hand—the better a person he tried to be, the better a songwriter he would be in the process, "And I've done some women wrong and had a lot of relationships in my life, some ups, some downs, some way ups, some way downs. I just know what it is they want, 'cause I know what it is they don't want." Perhaps based in part on his own disappointments caused to the women in his life over the years, Kelly also touched on the subject of loss, beyond that of his mother, in his songwriting on the R. album, citing "A Woman's Threat" as an example where "that [song is] trying to warn myself and other guys out there that if you got a good woman, try to hold on to her. Try to treat her right. Try your best."

Still, Kelly, even on this seemingly selfless topic, couldn't shake his penchant for patting his own back, congratulating himself on his progress in better understanding women, namely by claiming to one journalist that women thanked him for relating to their psyche so well, "[women come up to me and say] 'Thank you, because you said everything I've been trying to say to these fools for the longest time.'" Kelly explained the maturity of his songwriting as being based on a conciliatory personal philosophy in which, based on what he viewed as a departure from the past, "I'm not afraid to admit when I'm wrong or when I've done wrong; that's how you come to do right eventually. You continue to admit your mistakes and try to make it better."

Kelly's biggest priority at the time in terms of how he spun himself to fans in light of his growing success and stature (and the implied higher personal standard) within the industry seemed to lay in his attempt to remain constantly humble and pious in his interviews and public profiles, painting himself to the public as a servant of his talent, and, therein, of God, but still as a person, no different from the next man and just as prone to mistakes. He appeared to be attempting the creation of a safety net of sorts in which to fall back on from the spotlight, and into the solace of being "just like the next man…People look at celebrities like they're not human sometimes…I'm just trying to live right. I'm just trying to do the right thing." Kelly may have taken care at the time to insert and reemphasize such a statement because he wasn't always doing so off-stage in the course of his ongoing struggle with alleged infidelities involving underage women. Still, publicly, R. Kelly was on top of his game.

His fourth album, R. debuted at # 1 on the Billboard R&B Album Chart, scored hits with his duet "I'm Your Angel" with Celine Dion, which topped the Billboard Hot 100 Singles chart, the Hot 100 Singles Sales chart for 6 weeks, and the Adult Contemporary chart for 12 weeks, and with solo hit "When a Woman's Fed Up." In February of 1999 at the Grammy Awards, Kelly received nominations for Best Pop Collaboration with Vocals ("I'm Your Angel" with Celine Dion) and Best R&B Performance by a Duo or Group with Vocal ("Lean On Me" with Kirk Franklin, Mary J. Blige, Bono, and Crystal Lewis). In June, he won 2 Soul Train Music Awards for Best R&B/Soul Album, Male (R.), and the Sammy Davis Jr. Entertainer of the Year Award.

In August, 1999, he was named R&B Artist of the Year at the Source Hip-Hop Music Awards. Kelly topped off the year, in December, 1999 by winning the Billboard Music Award for R&B/Hip-Hop Artist of the Year. He even found time to give back to his community, establishing an inaugural "I Believe I Can Fly" celebrity basketball game in late 1997 (held annually thereafter), which benefited his childhood Chicago neighborhood on the South Side. In addition to featuring Washington Wizards' star Juwan Howard (who had grown up in the same impoverished section of the city as Kelly) as celebrity coach, Kelly underwrote the attendance of over 2,500 inner city residents to watch the game.

In a show of his artistic maturity and growing entrepreneurial savvy, Kelly, who had parted ways with longtime manager Barry Hankerton in 1998, also established his own record label, Rockland Records, distributed through Hip-Hop magnet Interscope Records, whose first commercial release, a debut by Kelly's protégé, Sparkle, scored platinum sales at retail, though it turned out to be an association which came back to haunt him when his video-taped sex scandal broke in early 2002. Still, at the time, Kelly spoke optimistically to journalists about Rockland's potential impact on the industry, excitedly describing the label's upcoming projects to include "a male trio called Talent. We just shot the video for their (debut) single "Celebrity." It's hot. These guys are very talented—they've got a lot of energy. I have another four-guy group coming out called Secret Weapon—same thing: very talented, real hard workers."

Additionally, Kelly, in interviews promoting his new label and album R., announced his intention to enter the realm of scoring and directing feature films. In all, Kelly felt he had grown substantially as both a composer and as an overall performer and artist, growth he clearly felt derived from the struggles he had endured over the course of his almost 10 years in the business.

As his empirical stature in the industry as the crossover king continually expanded through collaborations with Hip-Hop's biggest stars, including the Notorious B.I.G., Nas, and P. Diddy, as well as traditional R&B acts like Toni Braxton, Whitney Houston, Boyz II Men, Changing Faces, Trin-I-Tee 5:7, Blaque, Kelly Price, Maxwell, and Jodeci's duo spinoff K-CI & JoJo, he always rooted his success in his songwriting craft, which Kelly explained as an ongoing process in which he'd "been through a lot since my first album. I know I had a lot to say…In the growing of your success, the more you grow. The more you go through…The more you have to write about."

As 1999 ended and 2000 commenced, Kelly had also racked up a slew of new awards, reflecting his ever-present status as an R&B superstar. In January of 2000, Kelly had won Favorite Male Soul/R&B Artist at the American Music Awards, and in February, was nominated for several Grammy Awards, including Best Male R&B Vocal Performance ("When a Woman's Fed Up"), Best R&B Album (R.), and Best Rap Performance by a Duo or Group ("Satisfy You" with P. Diddy, which had hit number one on the charts for three weeks.) Additionally, Kelly won the Soul Train Music Award for Best R&B/Soul or Rap Album for his 1998 release R. in March of 2000.

As excitement over the millennium mounted, Kelly decided for his next album to host a celebration of his own, marking a decade in the business. Toward that end, Kelly released his 5th album, a boldly erotic and more old-school flavored collection entitled TP-2.COM, short for Twelve Play 2000. Kelly described the concept behind the record, surprisingly, more as a look at human relationships over sexual ones, "This album is pretty much about relationships more than sexual situations…Even though you have your choice of sexual songs on the album, you've got a lot of relationship situations on the album, also. By this being Twelve Play 2000, you have to back that up with some sexual songs of some sort."

Still, many critics caught on immediately to what most felt TP-2.COM was really about at heart, as evinced by Amazon.com's review of the record which stated in its first two lines that "the first single off of R. Kelly's TP-2.COM, "I Wish," might be a moving memorial to a dead friend, but the main theme on his latest CD is sex. The first tip-off that Kelly has left the spirit world to concentrate on nookie." To promote the album, Kelly set up a website, TP-2.com, and released a DVD retrospective of the same title, featuring a collection of his entire video catalog as well as rare interviews and back stage footage. Producing the top 40 hits "I Wish," "The Storm Is Over Now," and "Fiesta," Kelly's fifth album entered the charts at # 1 in November of 2000 at both the Billboard Top 200 Album chart and the Billboard R&B/Hip-Hop Chart, and was certified double platinum a month after its release, in December, 2000.

While the album featured touching odes to Kelly's late mother, including "Sadie" and "I Wish," which one reviewer described as "the project's most affecting track [and] emblematic of Kelly's [musical] sensibilities, "The track listing was predominantly Populated with titles like "The Greatest Sex," "Strip For You," "Feelin' on Your Booty," "Like a Real Freak," and the seminal title cut, "TP-2," whose first verse spoke in spirit of the album's overall fixation, "Hit it hard from the back / Roll around on the front / I know you've heard a lot of tracks / But 12 Play is what you want / Just let me call the studio / Then we can go all night / Girl I hope you can hang / Cause I'm horny as hell tonight."

To compliment the record's raunchy return to Kelly's vintage sound, a thematic world tour was planned, which Kelly excitedly described in preparation as "the 'Get Up On A Room' Tour…My band just flew in a week ago, so I'm letting them get familiar with the songs and just have jam sessions and stuff like that. But me and my cousin, Black, who's an A&R man at my record label, Rock Land, we're just vibing and coming up with these little gimmicks and gadgets. We got Busta [Rhymes], we got Foxy [Brown], we're talking to Nas, we have Deborah Cox, Sparkle, Kelly Price, and myself [headlining]."

The album was a hit on the awards circuit as 2001 began to unfold, with Kelly's nomination in February, 2001 for a Grammy for Best Male R&B Vocal Performance ("I Wish"), in March, won 2 Soul Train Music Awards for Best R&B/Soul Single, Male ("I Wish"), and Best R&B/Soul Album, Male (TP.2.COM), that same month winning 2 NAACP Image Award for Outstanding Male Artist and Outstanding Music Video.

In June of 2001, Kelly again hit chart gold with "Fiesta" (the first in what would become an album-long collaboration the next year with Jay Z), with the hit charting atop the Billboard R&B/Hip-Hop Singles & Tracks chart for 5 weeks, and the R&B/Hip-Hop Airplay chart for a week. With TP-2.COM, Kelly took it from Heaven back downstairs below the waistline, and even though the musical sophistication of the album was remarkable, it was clear where his mind was at with the record's lyrical content as well as with his complimentary off-stage antics.

Like a struggling addict or alcoholic who fell off the wagon, Kelly, following what appeared to be a period of personal serenity that was highlighted by his settling down and starting a family, had been drawn back into the illicit honey pit in 1999, when he, while on the video set for "If I Could Turn Back the Hands of Time," met a 17-year-old high school senior who was acting as an extra in the shoot.

Via an assistant who gave the girl Kelly's number, he began what the girl would later characterize as aggressive advances (despite his alleged knowledge of her age) that she described as beginning by "his assistant [giving] me his number, and from there we just started talking over the phone...I had told him the truth [about my age]—I don't believe in lying—but he was trying to woo me out there [to Chicago] despite the fact. Once I brought up the whole thing of, 'Well, I have to ask my mother,' he was like, 'You told your mom? Well, just wait then.'

"Despite the fact that Kelly chose to wait until the girl turned 18 to sleep with her, in the interim, he allegedly engaged in phone sex with the girl. Additionally, she claimed he told her he felt they were soul mates and that he was in love with her. The fact that Kelly was apparently ready and willing to commit adultery with the woman, and, according to her, did just that upon her turning 18, signals that he was already suffering serious setbacks in his judgment which the girl termed to be a result of what she characterized as "some kind of sexual problem." While the girl has since said she ended the relationship upon learning that Kelly was married, she also has expressed serious regret in falling for Kelly's advances at such a young and impressionable age, "I look back at it now and I think I was stupid; why the hell did I even go out there at all? There are some couples that there is a big age difference [and it's OK], but in this situation, I think that he really does have some kind of sexual problem. When I was flying out there he was like, 'You need to act older. There's 15 year old girls who act like they're 21 years old.' And I was like, 'Oh really? I'm not that old, and even if I was 30 years old, I'm not that type of person who's sticking their booty out, I'm sorry.'"

Matters worsened for Kelly when he allegedly became involved with an aspiring 17-year-old Rapper and former Epic Records intern named Tracy Sampson (professional name: Royalty), whom he allegedly began a sexual affair with in April, 2000 that lasted through March, 2001, according to a lawsuit that the Rapper filed against Kelly in August, 2001. According to the suit, details of the underage affair included Kelly's taking her virginity, "[coercing] her into receiving oral sex from a girl...[Expressing that] he was 'in love with her' and wished to continue with what she deemed] 'an indecent sexual relationship.'"

During the course of the affair, Kelly allegedly spoiled Sampson with what her suit claimed were "significant amounts of money... special access to recording studios and artists," and an all-expense paid trip to the Florida Super Bowl in 2001. In the course of her deposition for the suit, Sampson characterized her treatment at Kelly's hands as abusive, sexually degrading, and controlling, wherein she was allegedly "treated as his personal sex object and cast aside ...Our sexual encounters would always involve me giving him oral sex. During our sexual encounters, he would make me do disgusting things like stick my finger up my butt...He often tried to control every aspect of my life, including who I would see and where I would go."

Kelly, at first, as with Tiffany Hawkins' case, attempted to downplay the significance of the relationship, characterizing Sampson only as a "casual acquaintance" who had been to his studio only a handful of times and with whom he had no sexual contact. Kelly's initial refusal to acknowledge the relationship only served to add insult to Sampson's injury, according to her suit, causing her "emotional depression [wherein] I get headaches whenever I see or hear Robert Kelly. I have problems sleeping and am tired. My self-esteem is low. I cry when I think about what he made me do."

Though Kelly would later settle the suit with the girl for an undisclosed amount and in exchange, once again, for her sealed testimony, he seemed to be back to his old tricks again almost ten years after they had begun and five years after he had pledged to correct what he had termed to be a mysterious pattern of behavior he was personally ashamed of in the light of God. Prior to settling the suit, in interviews conducted during the release of TP-2.COM in 2000, Kelly remarked more than once to reporters that he was still in the midst of a personal struggle, presumably with infidelity, as he reasoned defensively in one interview that "there are two sides to all of us. Everybody's struggling with something. Nobody's perfect."

The levy began to crack publicly in 2000, despite Kelly's best efforts otherwise, when the *Chicago Sun-Times* ran an expo chronicling Kelly's alleged exploits with underage women. At the time, the story was largely dismissed as circumstantial, and would not be authenticated until over a year and a half later when the dam broke fully with the news that Kelly's underage trysts were caught on tape. Kelly attempted to further flesh out his struggle to fans in the year or so preceding the tape's unearthing by explaining that in some fundamental way, he seemed to find himself almost helpless to his obsession with women, such that he was willing to acknowledge so on record, "I'm not perfect. I see women every day and they are fine. I am like, `Wow.' I'm human. I'm a man. I grew up that way. The same with women. They see men. They like them and they go after them or they will look. Just as women may do me, I do them the same way and I embrace the love that they have for me. I embrace it."

Chapter 8

"Best of Both Worlds"

"'Jay-Z and R. Kelly together? Shit, that's pure 88 base right there!' shouts Rand 50, an amped kid with dollar signs in his eyes. 'I guarantee that album is going to do crack money like it's 19motherfucking88.'"

—*Vibe Magazine*

Best of Both Worlds should have been one of the best selling albums of the new millennium's first offering of superstar releases. Billed as a collaborative effort between New York Hip-Hop mogul and former crack dealer Jay Z, who throughout the latter 1990s had risen to become one of Rap's most prolific and preeminent forces as both an emcee and as co-owner/operator of Def Jam Recordings co-venture Roc-A-Fella Records, and R. Kelly, who at the time was still considered throughout the industry and world as one of R&B's biggest acts.

The buzz surrounding the duo's association began with their teaming up on the Kelly track "Fiesta," and the Jay Z track "Guilty Till Proven Innocent," and developed thereafter into a kinship that Kelly described as based both on mutual respect, artistic admiration, and a commonality in background that made one artist's vision for the project a reflection of the other's in terms of both its artistic fabric and commercial potential, "It only takes but a few seconds to establish a relationship with somebody real. So they knew I was real with mine, and they were real with theirs, so we bonded right there. 'Cause we all come from the same 'hood, just not the same city, and we go through the same things, so we kind of felt each other...I've worked with Jay-Z in the past so I know him. I know a lot of these Rap guys because in the industry you run into each other. But we didn't only run into each other, we had relationships and conversations."

Jay Z's recollection of the project's inspiration, while less passionate than Kelly's, was equally as enthusiastic and clearly based in mutual respect, "I can't really say when it started...We did "Fiesta," and "Guilty Until Proven Innocent," and it was like, 'Man, those records came out crazy, holmes.' We threw the idea of doing an album together back and forth, and before I knew it [it happened]." Both artists had a lot riding on the project, not only in that Best of Both Worlds was the first of its kind, as never before had a rapper of Jay Z's or R&B star of Kelly's stature teamed up for an entire album without being part of a group, but more importantly in the fact that because of their respective commercial positions within the industry, expectations were unusually high given past record sales. Def Jam Records President Lyor Cohen chalked the excitement up to something resembling a fixed horse race where all bets on the record were a sure thing, "People are going fucking bananas for this shit!...This is like throwing a cow into the piranha-filled Amazon! This is full-fledged pandemonium!...Jay told me to fasten my seat belt and watch this shit go down!"

In another groundbreaking move, because both artists were signed to separate labels, Jay Z to Def Jam Recordings, and R. Kelly to Jive Records, the question of who would distribute the record in the U.S. and Canadian territories hung in the air as recording got underway, potentially proving a sticking point in the vein of the

Tyson/Lewis Title match that was negotiated between the HBO and ShowTime cable networks. Fortunately, because relations were friendly across the board, Def Jam Recordings President Lyor Cohen, and Jive Records boss Barry Weiss decided the answer via a simple coin toss, which Cohen won by calling heads, allowing Def Jam to distribute the record with a even 50/50 split of profits down the line. Had he known the hailstorm of controversy to come that would plague and ultimately ruin the album's chances for the success everyone had already banked on, Cohen might have initially given Weiss the ball to run with.

Still, without the benefit of a crystal ball beyond the seemingly reliable predictions concerning the album's sales potential based on the stellar reputations of both performers at the time, Def Jam was looking forward to what they were sure would be another multi-platinum album hanging on their office walls. Kelly was equally as pumped for what he expected to be a sure platinum success, especially because the release would be counted as Kelly's next official album release following 2000's TP-2.COM. Given the 5-plus million copies the former album had sold, Kelly was rightfully enthused and expectant of a sequel in retail sales, "The expectations of what this album will be are so fucking high we'll probably never meet them…We started bragging, the best of R&B, the best of Rap. Let's put it together and see what happens…I've had niggas come up to me talking about, 'That's seven million off the top.'"

Best of Both Worlds was considered more of a vanity project for Jay Z given that being considered Rap's most prolific performer since Tupac Shakur had released an average of a full-studio album a year, all of which had gone multi-platinum since his debut in 1996, while Kelly tended to lapse 2 years between each release. With the Hip-Hop star's fan base solidly intact, Kelly had more vested in the project as he was seeking to increase his street credibility through the collaboration as well as expand his crossover sales among the traditional Hip-Hop audience.

In that respect, the album was a bold step for Kelly who had gone so far in one interview with *Vibe Magazine* as to term the album the potential "ghetto Thriller." That Kelly considered himself a thug was something of a headline to his traditional R&B fan base, who had for years past been used to his combination of erotic and religious anthems, arguably viewing Kelly as raunchy, but never as a gangsta. Still, Kelly was clearly ready to declare himself as such on the collaboration with Jay Z, apparently already feeling that his fans had connected with him to some degree on that level, "I think that people look at me sort of like a Rapper, but I just happen to sing. Because if Jay-Z was a singer, he would have written 'Down Low,' the remix. I'm just telling true stories, and talking about real things, and what goes on, like in 'When A Woman's Fed Up.' I take time with those and make sure that everything's right on point, so when people hear my song, they don't just hear the song and groove to it — they can actually picture it, almost like a movie on tape. And that's the way I like to write, to let people feel and see what's really happening in my life or in the life of somebody I know. I like people to listen to my stuff and say, 'Man, that just happened to me the other day!'"

With this among many other points of excitement and expectations hanging in the air, a national news conference was scheduled in the Spring of 2002 to publicize the street date for the album, which had already been moved up due to massive bootlegging, accounting for almost a quarter-million illegally manufactured copies of the album already moved on the street. Present at the news conference, which was held at the historic Waldorf-Astoria Hotel in New York, were many of Hip-Hop's biggest names, including P. Diddy and Russell Simmons, clearly in an effort to set the tone of the conference toward Rap's realm, to present a more street-savvy edge to the event, and possibly to allow Kelly some pre-release exposure in that light.

Sadly, despite the generally strong buzz surrounding the release, its potential commercial impact was already damaged by critics who were taking the album less seriously than Kelly would have liked, likening it to more of a party record than anything that could be as influential as many of the artists' individual career releases like Jay Z's seminal debut "Reasonable Doubt," or Kelly's "12 Play." A prime example of the latter was the review that Hot 97.1, New York's premier Hip-Hop radio station, gave the album in advance of its street date, and prior to the Kelly scandal breaking. The review painted the album as "full of good ideas gone wrong, untapped potential and miscasting... packed with ego, wrapped in narcissism, and gilded with indifference." The review went on to focus on Kelly's attempts to be taken seriously as a thug, making fun at what they termed Kelly "[waving] his thug bandanna, [singing] with potty-mouthed glee and [dropping] lines such as 'Some of y'all niggas mad 'cause I drop these hits/Thug-ass nigga on some R&B shit.'"

Ultimately, the influential radio station, like many critics, concluded the album as something of an artistic masturbation piece for both performers, accomplishing not much more than a few outstanding moments of euphoria before becoming something of a disappointment based on what critics and fans alike had been expecting, coupled with what artists of both Jay Z and Kelly's respective talents could have been capable of, "More than anything, The Best of Both Worlds is a showcase for Jay and Kelly to revel in their own celebrity...far from the musical epic these men are probably capable of making together."

Still, based on the number of bootlegged albums that had been moved on the streets of urban music centers like New York and Chicago, industry analysts were able to make a fairly favorable forecast for the album among both artists' traditional fan bases that put the album's first week sales somewhere in the million-selling range. As the record approached release in the early spring of 2002, *Vibe Magazine* echoed similar predictions, proclaiming in a feature on the forthcoming release that "it's safe to say that Best of Both Worlds—produced by Kelly and Tone of Track Masters and featuring Lil' Kim, Beanie Sigel, Boo & Gotti—will be one of 2002's most sought-after albums."

Kelly, by late 2001, had been made aware of the existence of a videotape allegedly showing him engaged in heated and explicit sexual intercourse with what appeared to most viewers, who, at this point, had been select journalists and law enforcement officials within the city's sex crimes investigation unit, to be a very young teenage girl. While the tape's existence had not yet made the headlines and the bootleg circuit nationwide, it could be argued from one point of view that Kelly made the tape, in anticipation of its impending release, because he was seeking to expand his listening audience into the realm of Hip-Hop because of the genre's traditionally higher tolerance for unsavory personal behavior among its performers, such as Best of Both Worlds teammate Jay Z, who had plead guilty in late 2001 to the stabbing of Record Executive Lance 'Un' Rivera at a New York night club and received three years probation.

Hip-Hop had built its platinum foundation on an ability to mirror the hell of the inner cities to the commercial masses, to the point where the genre's stars, big and small, were effectively ghetto politicians national representatives of their respective local communities and citizenry. As a result, it was the accepted and expected norm by the new millennium that Hip-Hop stars should have some sort of authentic criminal background on which to authenticate the urban struggles they were speaking about on record, establishing, and in many cases adding actively to, their street credibility among record buyers.

Popular topics that Rappers touched on typically included requisite topics like poverty, single-mother households, narcotic sales, gang affiliations, routine run-ins with the police, and on occasion, more violent crimes including murder. Death Row Records—helmed by gang-affiliated and convicted felon CEO Marion 'Suge' Knight and marquee stars Snoop Dogg and Tupac Shakur (the latter of whom, at his commercial peak, had racked up a lengthy Rap sheet of convictions encompassing many of the aforementioned categories)— had revolutionized the gangster formula in the 1990s, making active criminal affiliations a norm within Hip-Hop. As a result in many cases, Rap stars were encouraged to indulge in the type of behavior and relationships that could potentially land them in trouble with the law, where previously they had been encouraged by success to leave such associations behind.

By the new millennium, the necessitated portrayal of an authentic gangster image on record and off and its inarguable impact on album sales, had become inextricably linked so much that the record buying-public were used to seeing their Hip-Hop heroes in legal trouble as an active reflection of what they, themselves, were going through day in and out. Authenticity was a bottom line, and the ghetto-fabulous lifestyle was routinely celebrated rather than shunned as it had been in years past.

Regardless of the fact that Hip-Hop stars usually got preferential treatment within the legal system due to both their celebrity and ability to finance top-dollar defenses and plea-agreements, their willingness to put their freedom and celebrity on the line in the name of keeping it real created loyalty among fans and typically worked to increase their album sales. This willing sacrifice had proved true for a host of multi-platinum Rap artists including the late Tupac Shakur and the Notorious B.I.G., Snoop Doggy Dogg (whose debut album had debuted at # 1 the week he was charged with first degree murder for his part in a gang-related drive-by shooting), DMX (who grew up largely in Juvenile Correctional institutions), and Jay Z (who was a notorious crack dealer in Brooklyn's Marcy Projects).

Unfortunately for Kelly—presuming his linking with Jay Z was partly designed to identify commercially with the rapper's fans in anticipation of the potential fallout when word of his sex tape hit the streets—the most he had ever been collared for was a misdemeanor arrest for violating a sound ordinance by playing his car stereo too loudly after hours in his hometown of Chicago. Additionally, the American public had already drawn its line of tolerance for celebrity indiscretions at murder (a ready example being O.J. Simpson) and child abuse (the most notorious example in recent years being Michael Jackson). Kelly was about to fall within the latter category and his early reaction to questions on the tape's existence was the most dangerous—defiance.

Kelly gave his first public response to the tape's alleged existence on February 8, 2002, more than a month before Best of Both Worlds scheduled March 19th release, as he was backstage preparing to go before a crowd of thousands to perform "The World's Greatest" at the Salt Lake City's Winter Olympics. Kelly's very presence at the event as a performer was a ready reflection of his commercial stature across multiple musical genres at the outset of the scandal that wildly rocked his insulated, superstar world. The reality that the tape's existence, in the midst of Kelly's very mainstream Popularity, pointed out the seriousness of his potential vulnerability was clearly present in the singer's mind as he angrily answered a journalist's question about the tape by flatly denying its authenticity while acknowledging the potential damage it could do to his legacy, "The world is getting ready to watch me sing…and you've got a tape out there trying to ruin my career…It's Rap, and that's how we're going to treat it."

Unfortunately, as word of the tape broke fast across the nation's airwaves, newspapers, and on-line gossip columns, it was immediately clear that the greater world was taking the contents of the tape a lot more seriously than R. Kelly would have preferred. Though Def Jam Records moved forward in releasing the long-awaited and much-hyped album on March 19th as scheduled, the impact of Kelly's breaking scandal was instantaneously evident in the record's poor first-week showing at retail, scanning a disappointing 230,000 copies (in light of the million-plus predictions of many industry insiders) and debuting on the Billboard Top 200 Album Chart, when Jay Z, and for the most part, Kelly had never been denied the coveted # 1 slot for the majority of their respective releases prior. Worse yet, Def Jam cancelled all touring, video, and print promotion for the album that had not already occurred, and Jay Z began to Rapidly distance himself from any potentially negative exposure or fall out within his own core fan base as Kelly's sex scandal began to captivate a gossip-hungry nation.

While the Rapper tried to be publicly polite and supportive of Kelly's unfolding drama, he was careful not to be overly diplomatic in his pledge, telling MTV that "I wished him luck and said 'Take care of yourself.'" Privately, most believed Jay Z was taking more aggressive and elaborate measures to insulate himself from Kelly's mess, including one example in which, according to *Time Magazine's* online website, "Jay Z, through an intermediary, thanked the editor of *Vibe Magazine* for removing him from [the] current cover with R. Kelly."

The record went on to be the biggest disappointment of either artist's careers, selling under 500,000 units and leaving Kelly's future as an R&B superstar and global sex symbol largely uncertain. Unfortunately, fan scrutiny was not the only negative reaction to the existence of the sex tape that Kelly had to concern himself with as the Chicago Police Department's Sex Crimes Unit soon brought judgment upon Kelly's alleged misconduct, threatening not only the singer's livelihood, but more importantly, his very freedom.

Chapter 9

"Sex, Lies, and Videotape"

"You suppose if someone were innocent they'd be ready to fight. But I want people to know that there's a difference when you're famous. And I wish I hadn't settled those. I can't do anything about that now, but my lawyers told me at the time that I should settle because I had a lot of things going on, some hits were out at the time and it was R. Kelly rising. And at that time those people came at me the lawyers said it was best for me not to go on with this because it could mess up my career or whatever, and now I regret that. I wish I would have fought. If it was today I'd fight that, I truly would fight that."

—R. Kelly to MTV's John Norris in May, 2002, denying that he has a fetish for underage women in the midst of his sex-tape scandal.

(Before hearing anymore of R. Kelly's denials—the tapes). In early spring, 2002, *Chicago Sun-Times* reporters Jim DeRogatis and Abdon Pallasch received a Fed Ex from an anonymous sender containing any reporter's wet dream: a 26-minute, 39 second videotaped celebrity scandal that was theirs alone to take public. Before using the tape in an exclusive, news breaking headline on its existence which read, in part, that "Chicago police are investigating whether R&B superstar R. Kelly—part of today's opening act at the Winter Olympics in Salt Lake City—had sex with an underage girl and videotaped the illegal act," which ran on February 8, 2002, the reporters turned the tape over to the Chicago Police, who, well prior to the story's airing, already had their Sex Crimes Unit investigating R. Kelly's alleged participation in multiple video-taped sexual encounters with what appeared to be an underage girl who some speculated was as young as 14 at the time of the tape filming.

As *Time Magazine* reported in March, 2002 following the Police Department's receipt of the tape, "Within weeks, the video landed on the internet and on bootleg tables across America's inner cities... now sold as R. Kelly Exposed." A brief synopsis of one of the many potentially criminal highlights from the tape, according to *Time's* report, included "a man who appears to be Kelly ejaculating and urinating on what appears to be an adolescent girl." *Spin Magazine*, in May, 2002, elaborated with its own revelations concerning the contents of the tape, reporting that "the 26-minute video begins with the man sitting on a bench in the center of the frame.

The action starts as his partner—a petite, fair-skinned black girl— halfheartedly gives him a blowjob. Naked except for a small gold cross across her neck, she proceeds to dirty-dance for him, then follows his instructions to relieve herself on the stone floor. Next, she straddles him, and they have sex while she calls him 'Daddy.' Finally, standing over her reclining form, the man urinates in the girl's mouth and over her breasts and stomach before fondling himself to climax...[An aunt confirmed that the] girl is 14 or 15 in the tape." Worse yet, despite the repeated denial and alleged conspiracies that came from Kelly's mouth, even through his lawyers implicating his own brother, most felt Kelly had been caught red-handed with his pants down, as *Time's* article pointed out that "the man [who allegedly is Kelly] peers directly into the camera several times and the scenes take place in a wood-paneled room that strongly resembles one in Kelly's house where the singer has posed for various magazine covers."

The fact that Kelly had allegedly filmed himself in his own home, more specifically in the very room where he had been known to invite journalists, rather than a more discrete place like his bedroom, which might have been harder to identify, implied that Kelly felt his privacy was completely intact at the time of the filming that he displayed a sense of intimacy and invulnerability on tape that lends itself strongly to the notion Kelly had no idea he would ever be caught in the act.

Worse yet, journalists quickly pinpointed the tape's filming as having occurred sometime between late 1998 and early 1999 at a time when Kelly was at his career heights and had claimed very publicly to have cleaned up his off-stage infidelities and settled down to raise a family, as identified by *Spin Magazine* in May, 2002, when they reported that " a television plays in the background through much of the clip, and the audible songs and TV commercials [including one for 'The Money Store,' which closed in 2000] suggest that the tape was made in late 1998 or early 1999." That he would have been engaging in adultery on top of what many were beginning to speculate were a variety of violations of Illinois' child pornography laws only made matters worse for Kelly personally, all in addition to the professional fall out that had already begun.

Aside from Jay Z's Rapid public distancing from Kelly, other industry heavyweights were already chiming in with opinions on the potential commercial impact for Kelly, with one industry insider, interviewed in the same Spin expo, who summed up where Kelly had potentially crossed the line by reasoning that while the public has a high tolerance for devious behavior among entertainers, "the thing a lot of people can't seem to get out of their minds this time is the image of a grown man peeing on a little girl. I don't care what anyone says—that doesn't sound like fun and games to me. It sounds like a man with a problem."

Legendary Hip-Hop producer Dr. Dre offered a potentially similar sentiment, telling MTV, "I've been hearing a lot of talk on the radio [in Los Angeles] from stations that are saying they're not going to play his records ever again because they saw the video and he's a sick bastard…But I don't know if it's true. I only know what I've heard. I haven't seen the video, nor do I want to see it because there's a kid involved. That's where I draw the line. You can do almost anything except touch kids or something like that. That's a no-no, you know what I'm saying? If he's guilty, he's over. I'm just waiting for the results."

In an effort to demonstrate a pattern as the investigation heated up, the Chicago Police also made the media aware of at least two additional videotapes that had been brought to their attention, allegedly showing Kelly engaging again and again in a variety of explicit sexual acts with women, none of whom were specifically identified as underage, but nevertheless, young enough in age to fit Kelly's alleged M.O. According to *Spin Magazine*, "In early 2001, a videotape began circulating that depicted Kelly receiving oral sex from a different light-skinned black girl in what looks like the same room seen in the video that surfaced recently. [Police are investigating the tape, but the age and identity of the girl have not been determined.] In late February of this year, a third video, purporting to show Kelly having sex with a teenage girl, briefly surfaced as a downloadable clip on the gossip website UrbanExpose.com; the clip was removed two days later. [An attorney representing Kelly maintains the tape is a fake; the website's owners did not respond to requests for comment.]"

Sadly, the more details of the alleged Kelly tape made their way public, the more graphic they became, such that, according to *Spin Magazine*'s dissection of the middle of the tape's contents, Kelly's guilt apparently becomes more vivid, as he appears "conscious of the camera at all times, periodically adjusting it to capture, among other acts, the perfect money shot…The girl doesn't look a day over 15. When he hands her what appears to be a crumpled-up wad of bills, she says, 'Thank you' and begins to perform fellatio. The tape then cuts to the naked girl dancing suggestively to the camera as songs by the Backstreet Boys and Spice Girls play in the background on MTV. Kelly, not on camera, can be heard moaning, 'Damn, baby.'…His moaning grows louder when the girl stops gyrating and begins urinating on the floor. Shortly afterward, the girl mounts Kelly cowgirl style, and at his behest begins to talk loudly to the camera. 'Oh fuck me, Daddy,' she cries. 'Is Daddy fucking you good?' the star asks repeatedly. Apparently, he's into water sports, because approximately 20 minutes into the tape, Kelly, standing over the girl, begins to urinate on her face and chest. The girl looks visibly uncomfortable for a moment but lays still. Shortly after relieving himself, he begins to masturbate and then ejaculates on the girl. He's kind enough to wipe the residue off with a towel."

By March, 2002, the public felt that enough sorted details of the tapes' contents had been revealed to turn attention to the identity of who exactly appeared in Kelly's alleged home videos. The Chicago Police already had what they felt was the girl's identity, but were withholding her identity due to her status as a minor. The media soon got an independent confirmation from the girl's aunt, Stephanie Edwards, a Kelly protégé who went by the professional name Sparkle, who had had a nasty falling out two years prior with the R&B superstar.

While, to date, it has not been established with certainty who leaked the tape to the Chicago Police and to the media, it was clear Sparkle was more than happy to cooperate with authorities, claiming that her niece was 12 at the time she was first introduced to Kelly, and that by 14, they were engaging in an illicit sexual affair. Sparkle spoke to MTV news as details of the scandal continued to emerge throughout the middle spring, chastising Kelly for his behavior, and expressing personal remorse over her sense of responsibility for putting her niece in the position to be seduced by Kelly, "She kept coming down with me…which was [a] safe [situation] at the time. But after R. and I parted ways, it was me not watching over her. So I feel a responsibility for that also, although I'm not responsible for his actions, I feel responsible for even taking her there….It's messed up. She's being exposed to the world. It's sickening… It's crazy and torn up, in every way imaginable…It's hurtful to my sister, to my brother-in-law and to my niece, especially, because it's all her."

The scorned performer even went as far as to identify for police and the media the exact location where she believed the taped sexual encounters took place, that being one of two identical wood-paneled rooms that Kelly had constructed at his Olympia Fields mansion, and his downtown Chicago high rise apartment. According to Sparkle, her niece had turned 17 in September of 2001, and while she had been interviewed twice by Chicago Police, denying both times that she was the woman on the tape, the Sex Crimes unit investigators appeared to be more interested in interviewing her parents, who had been sent on vacation in Europe in mid-December, 2001, allegedly on Kelly's dime.

In an article titled "Teenager's parents eyed in R. Kelly case," run in the *Chicago Tribune* in June, 2002, the paper reported that, "State child-welfare officials said they have reopened their probe into whether the parents of an underage girl left her in the care of R&B star R. Kelly knowing the two would engage in sexual activity…In December, the Illinois Department of Children and Family Services received a tip that the parents of the girl—who police say was video-taped having sex with the singer—knew Kelly 'would engage in sexual activity with her,' said agency spokeswoman Martha Allen."

Additionally, while Sparkle's niece denied in both interviews to both Chicago Police and state child-welfare workers that she was the girl featured on the tape, in late Spring, 2002, as investigators were nearing the filing of formal charges against Kelly, it was reported via the Police department and confirmed in the *Chicago Tribune*, that forensic experts had concluded the girl was in fact the one present in what was allegedly Kelly's home video.

Kelly's denials began with one of his attorneys, John M. Touhy, who was the first to suggest the tape might be doctored, remarking to one reporter that, "Mr. Kelly is at the top of his career…He has a hit song out right now, he performed at the NFC title game, and he's performing at the Olympics. In light of those events, I believe you have to have serious questions in your mind about the motives of people who sent…that forged tape." Kelly went public in May, 2002 with interviews on BET and MTV denying his presence on the tape as well as any larger problem with underage women, and attempted to flesh out his theory on why Sparkle had lodged such fallacious allegations at him, acknowledging that, Sparkle has a very good reason to be mad at me right now. We had a business relationship and it didn't work out because she wanted to have somebody else produce her after her first album was a hit, and I just didn't understand that. It's not an ego thing, but I'm the top, I'm one of the top producers out here, and I told her, 'I produced this and I'm not gonna let somebody else produce your album. I'm producing your album.' And it became a very big deal, and I believe a big part of it was that she was in a relationship with this producer, and it started going downhill ever since. She started thinking that I'm trying to tell her what to do in the next album and she quit, she left the company and her career went downhill. I've gotten little threats from her and now she hates me and it's my fault." Kelly even went as far as acknowledging that he knew the girl allegedly pictured on the tape, telling MTV's John Norris that while he had something of a relationship with her, it was plutonic, and that she herself had denied it was anything more, "I was like a godfather to her… She denied it. Her mom and her dad denied it. And a few other people that have seen it have denied it."

Still, Kelly was left largely to lodging flimsy and desperate charges of conspiracy in explaining away the presence of the multiple videos, arguing to one MTV journalist that "I have an ex-manager that's been on my back [Hankerton denied Kelly's allegation, stating flatly that, 'I have never seen the tape and have nothing to do with Mr.

Kelly's problems.']…A lot of people know about it, but when the smoke clears, you guys will really be able to know exactly what is going on…People are trying to make money off my music and my name in a very, very negative way. I've been blackmailed for the last four years, and I didn't give in, and I'm still not gonna give in… There are a lot of people who are very jealous of me right now…and they're trying to destroy me…People are trying to bring me down."

When pressed for more specific details of the alleged conspiracy, Kelly hid behind his lawyers throughout several interviews, explaining that, "From the beginning I wanted to speak—believe me, I was gritting my teeth every time I would hear something negative about me or something that's not true about me. It hurt me and I wanted to say something really bad, but, unfortunately, even now I have one hand tied behind my back.…I can't just name names. Just the regular guy Robert wants to, but I have to follow some advice." He further alleged that the tape's surfacing was part of a larger effort by unnamed parties to extort money from Kelly, "I don't think this is over because it started something that's just unbelievable. Everybody is calling. Some people call now but they don't call back after the lawyer tells them to go screw themselves. They don't call back. Some call back. Some don't call back. Some call back and keep calling then they don't call back no more. Some are calling and they're not going away… This other thing that's at me now, people claiming whatever they're claiming, I'm fighting it. I'm not settling that because I feel like I keep settling things and it's like everybody is coming out of the woodwork trying to get paid."

Kelly was clear in pointing out that he had no desire to see the tape he was allegedly pictured throughout, telling MTV's John Norris that, "I have no interest in seeing anything that I know I haven't done. It would make me look bad to go look at something that is not me… it doesn't make sense for me to want to see something that is not me. First of all, if it's as disgusting as people say it is and as crazy as people say it is…I have no interest in seeing some man with a woman whether she's underage or not underage, I have no interest in that."

Still, despite his best denials, within the context of his interviews prior to being formally charged the next month in June, 2002, where after Kelly ceased public comment altogether, he tried to bring the current allegations against him into perspective by conceding that, concerning his battling a problem with infidelity, which based on the time the tapes were filmed, he seemed clearly guilty of, "I've been battling this storm for a long time… I've been crying for a long time even in my music… I'm already embarrassed. It's out there and everybody knows it's R. Kelly day…This whole rumor thing has really pushed me to change my music." While Kelly was still focused on his career in a positive light, the larger question of whether his fans were remained unanswered.

Early indications based on the poor performance of his collaborative album with Jay Z, Best of Both Worlds, suggested a poorer commercial outlook for R. Kelly's future. Still, the singer remained defiant of the latter prediction, arguing that "I know that my fans believe in me. They still play my music. My music is still selling. That lets me know that this situation didn't affect that. But I believe that people got into my personal business in the studio and got a Best of Both Worlds CD maybe six months before the project came out and started bootlegging it, big time. If there were a way we could check the bootlegging, I believe it would be the biggest bootlegging situation in history." In a further effort to try to reel at least some of his core fan base back in, Kelly released a single in the summer of 2002 entitled "Heaven I Need a Hug," which included the lyrics "Heaven I Need a Hug / Is there anyone out there who will embrace a thug?"

The Chicago Police Department agreed with Kelly's assessment of himself as a 'thug' as they quietly prepared a criminal complaint against Kelly over the course of May, 2002. On Wednesday, June 6,

2002, embattled R&B star R. Kelly was arrested on a fugitive nationwide $750,000 warrant issued via Chicago in Davenport, outside Orlando, in Polk County, Florida, approximately 20 miles from Disneyland, as he was preparing to leave a rented vacation home where he had lived for more than a year with his wife and three children, to drive back to Chicago, where his attorney had apparently made arrangements for Kelly to turn himself in to authorities.

Before he could hit the road, however, Kelly was taken into custody by Florida authorities and processed (possibly fearing him as a flight risk). Following his being held overnight in the County lock-up in isolation, Kelly posted more than $150,000 bail before being released to travel back to Chicago, which occurred following what his lawyer characterized as time to "get his composure, as soon as he sees his wife and kisses his babies, as soon as he puts on a new set of clothes and is able to get a few hours' sleep." Among the terms of his Florida bail bond, Kelly was barred from having contact with children unrelated to him by blood or marriage.

According to E-Online.com, Kelly arrived "by private plane [Thursday] morning and was taken by silver Lexus to the Cook County Criminal Courts Building...[Kelly] was [immediately] approached by police, who read him his rights, cuffed him and whisked him to a nearby precinct house for booking...About 45 minutes later, after being fingerprinted and having his mug shot taken, Kelly posted a $75,000 cash bond (which is 10 percent of the $750,000 stipulated by his arrest warrant) and left via the Lexus," according to his lawyer Ed Genson, "to go home and sleep."

Kelly was charged with 21 counts of child pornography, wherein, according to E-Online.com, "The indictment, handed down Wednesday morning, [included] seven counts of videotaping the sex act with a minor, seven counts of producing the video and seven counts of soliciting or enticing the minor to engage in the illicit sex acts…charging that Kelly 'knew or should have known that the girl was born in September of 1984, and, therefore, was a minor at the time of the sex acts.'" The charges faced Kelly with up to15 years and a fine of up to $100,000.

While Chicago Police Superintendent, Terry Hillard, Chief of Detectives, Phil Cline, and a host of fellow investigators and prosecutors were holding a press conference explaining that, "The fact that children and communities have been harmed as a result of [Kelly's] actions is very, extremely important to us," and terming Kelly's celebrity as "of no importance to us", Kelly's lead attorney, Ed Genson, was busy lambasting the police for reneging on what he claimed had been an agreement wherein Kelly would be allowed to travel back to Chicago to face the music voluntarily, "I've represented congressmen, I've represented judges, I've represented people charged in all sorts of offenses, and I've never had an agreement like this breached…I don't know whether it's his race, I don't know whether it's his celebrity, but we were double-crossed…I felt it was an attempt to portray Robert as someone who wasn't willing to come in, as some sort of fugitive."

Kelly released a statement Thursday afternoon defending his innocence and stating that, "Even though I don't believe any of these charges are warranted, I'm grateful that I will have a chance to establish the truth about me in a court of law. I have complete faith in our system of justice, and I'm confident that when all the facts come out, people will see that I'm no criminal."

Kelly's attorney elaborated on Kelly's statement by explaining to the Associated Press that, from the defense's perspective, "The charge is that there's a young lady under the age of 18 on that tape and there isn't…That's simply the stance that I'm taking." The Chicago Police obviously begged to differ, and cited an extremely lengthy and elaborate investigation into the tape's background and authenticity to support their position in filing charges against Kelly. So much so that, according to CNN.com, the Chicago police "interviewed more than 50 witnesses who went before the grand jury and identified the singer as the person in the video, authorities said. The FBI crime lab in Quantico, Virginia, authenticated the tape, officials said."

With the charges against Kelly now public, his arrest (including both mug shots) having made headlines internationally, everyone from music critics to journalists to civil rights groups began sounding off with their opinions, either in support of or against Kelly's cause. This laundry list included community activists like Philadelphia-based Racial Unity, whose lead activist, Asa Khalif, lead an organized boycott of Kelly's latest release, Best of Both Worlds, citing outrage at the videotape's contents as his group's, who represented homosexual African Americans, motivation, "The tape I saw had one young girl who had to be 13 or 14 years old…The look of anguish and shame on her face was enough for me to say, 'This is wrong.'"

R&B rival Sisqo, of the group Dru Hill, who had had a Kelly-derivative hit the previous summer with "Thong Song," came out on record against Kelly with "This is Heart" which featured the lyrics "Let me remind you of that shit you did / The 'world's greatest'? Whatever / Ain't nothing but a child molester." Other industry insiders offering opinions included Axis Music Group co-founder Vikter Duplaix, who produced such R&B hit acts as The Roots and Erykah Badu, reasoned that even if Kelly was guilty, he could still recover in time as "the [African-American] community is very forgiving…But it really comes down to how he handles himself after he comes back, because it's such a dark thing to [abuse] children."

With all the media attention and gossip surrounding the tape also came curiosity among the American public to see for themselves, causing sales of the bootlegged tape to skyrocket. The Police paid particular attention to this phenomenon when they held their initial press conference to coincide with Kelly's arrest, pointing out to all listening ears that, "It would be my advice to you to dispose of these tapes [as they are now considered child pornography.]"

Some tried to point the blame at the *Chicago Sun-Times*, the original recipient of the tape, for turning it over to the police in the first place, thus acting as a catalyst for the tape's wide bootlegging in addition to suggesting that doing so was a violation of the journalistic principle of protecting sources. Still, the paper argued that it was obligated by law to turn over the tape since it depicted what appeared to be an illegal act, and that since they had not revealed the source of the tape, who they did not even know, the *Tribune* was covered. As *Sun-Times'* Vice-President of Editorial further explained, "There is no principle that says the press is not obliged to act in the public interest…Because of the appearance of the commission of a crime, we felt obliged to do something about that…. We're on the side of justice. That's what this newspaper is about. We're not natural enemies of anybody else."

While the public was buzzing and brewing up theory and speculation on how the case would play out for Kelly in both the legal and commercial arenas, the embattled R&B star was privately beginning to plot his defense with attorneys. Kelly's first step was to apologize to his fans, telling MTV's John Norris in an interview that, "I want to apologize to my fans for all of this and thank them for being there for me through thick and thin. Because even in the past my fans have always been there for me and I just want to ask them to focus on my music and don't focus on this, just focus on the music, focus on my talent, and get through this with me. And I want to ask people out there to pray for me, not just that I come through this situation, but that I be the man that I want to be and a better person."

While Kelly was out playing contrite in public, in private, his lawyers were going through every possible theory of potential defense for their client in the face of the F.B.I.-authenticated videotape. Where Kelly's attorneys had, prior to the singer being arrested and indicted, charged publicly that the videotape was in fact a fake, that it had been doctored, and that its existence was part of some larger conspiracy by unidentified persons to extort money from Kelly, most notable was when one of his lead attorneys, John M. Touhy, stated flatly that "I believe you have to have serious questions in your mind about the motives of people who sent you that forged tape" early on in 2002.

That defense quickly fizzled when it became clear that the police had indicted based on authentications from both state and federal forensics experts, who had, to the Police's satisfaction, established the identities of both Kelly and Ms. Edwards' niece. Kelly's lead attorney, Ed Genson, now was adopting a different strategy, one that simple involved his disproving that the girl on the tape was underage, and, therein, making the foundation of the charges crumble as mute, "We're going to court and we'll disprove that she was underage." Cook County State's Attorney, Richard Devine, retorted publicly with an equal simplicity of Kelly's lawyer that, "We would not have proceeded if we weren't confident with the identification of the people on the tape."

Chapter 10

"My Brother's Keeper"

With the evidence against Kelly stacking against him, his defense appeared to become more desperate by the day. Kelly had first attempted to suggest the tape was doctored—authorities blew that theory out of the water via forensic authentication. Forensic identification of both audio and video, known as video image analysis, is an extremely defined science in which the Federal Bureau of Investigation is considered among the field's foremost experts. According to videosurveillanceexpert.com, a leading expert in the field of video surveillance and authentication (ironically representing Kelly in his defense), offered on their website a partial list of the F.B.I.'s process for authenticating videotapes, involving an extremely thorough set of procedures in which the "forensic examinations of videotapes usually consist of both a visual and aural examination.

One of the more important pieces of equipment used in forensic video examinations is a waveform monitor which is a specialized oscilloscope. It displays the voltage versus time modes and has specialized circuits to process the signal... Additional tests include measurements of the chrominance, hue and burst of the color videotape by using a vector scope... Lastly, [to investigate possible] videotape editing, the examination will require a frame-by-frame inspection, with the use of waveform monitors, vector scopes, and a cross pulse monitor together with other forensic equipment as deemed appropriate."

Once Kelly's legal team realized their first and arguably silliest line of defense, the 'forgery' claim, held little chance of being taken seriously by a jury, they next attempted to back off of their initial rebuff of the tape's authenticity by acknowledging that it could, in fact, be their client on the tape. Even so, he still wasn't guilty because now, they claimed, all of the women filmed, including the one who the F.B.I. and Chicago Police identified as being between 14 and 15 at the time, were in fact of age and over 18 at the time the tape was shot, making them all consenting adults.

Due to their increasing awareness of the likelihood that this defense wouldn't hold much water either since the police had positively identified the alleged victim in the tape as Stephanie Edwards' niece as a minor, Kelly's third shift in legal strategy would mark his saddest and most desperate moment yet. As the media frenzy died down in the weeks following Kelly's formal arrest and arraignment on child pornography charges, a more focused stream of reporting began to emerge as preliminary hearings were attended, and motions filed. Among these, one stood out as a notable shift in legal direction for Kelly's defense and exposed itself for the slick but desperate ploy in the summer of 2002, when Kelly's attorneys introduced a videotape from the Judge Mathis television program that featured Kelly's younger brother, Carey Kelly, in what many speculated was becoming an attempt on R. Kelly's part to suggest that the male featured on the tape in question was in fact his brother, Carey, rather than the singer himself.

As reported through the Associated Press, "Rumor has it that Robert Kelly's defense attorneys are looking to argue how it could be Carey Kelly—and not R. Kelly on the sex tape at the center of the criminal investigation, and thus cast doubt on the charges against the singer. That rumor was taken seriously enough that prosecutors subpoenaed an episode of the Judge Mathis Show in which Carey Kelly had appeared, apparently to evaluate the resemblance on videotape between the two." What made this latest ploy so sad was that Kelly, appearing to have run out of viable excuses and denials, had sunk low enough to resort to attempting to implicate his brother, who had gone on record already emphatically denying that he was pictured, or for that matter, had ever been to the residence where the tape was filmed. According to Carey Kelly who gave an interview to the *Chicago Sun-Times* shortly following the hearing, "The person on the tape is not me…If need be, I am willing to take a lie detector test to prove that it is not me. I feel that my character is being damaged." Carey more passionately denied his affiliation in any way, shape, or form with his brother's alleged taped trysts, stating outright that, "No dollar amount in the world would get me to [take the Rap for him]…I've got kids. Not a dollar in the world could buy my soul."

While Kelly's defense appeared to be gearing up for a legal strategy in which a jury might buy into this attempted assertion, Kelly's brother certainly wasn't ready to play patsy. In interview after interview, he emphatically denied his appearance on the tape, systematically breaking down the logic to such a below-the-belt move on his brother's part. To begin with, Carey was careful to separate himself from his brother in terms of their off-stage pastimes. While R. Kelly's younger brother had toured with him as a member of the R&B star's dance troupe from 1990 through 1996, a period R. Kelly has readily described as his wildest off-stage, Carey was quick to point out that his relationship with R. Kelly, even during that time, was more professional than personal in nature, such that "sometimes [on tour] I wouldn't see him until we hit the stage, I stayed at different hotels sometimes…There's a lot of private things going on."

In elaborating on his relationship with his brother in the years following his touring with R. Kelly, younger brother Carey offered several more significant revelations that went toward refuting the very foundation of any argument on Kelly's defense's part that Carey could have ever been the man pictured in the tapes.

Topping Carey's list of rebuttals to Kelly's potential line of defense was the fact that he had never even been to the homes in which R. Kelly's videos were allegedly shot. Because both the media and the police had been able to pinpoint the exact room in Kelly's residences, a pair of identical wood-paneled sauna rooms where the authorities felt the underage sexual encounters had been filmed, Carey would have had to have had ready and comfortable access to the homes as well as a familiarity with those specific locations within the domiciles to have been the man pictured in the tapes. Moreover, because of the intimate nature of the encounters, the man filmed would have to have been warmly familiar with the room, feeling it was private enough to exist completely in the nude through the entirety of the videos, know the precise location of what appeared to be a hidden camera, and to engage in extremely explicit sexual situations with multiple women. Still, according to Carey, "I've never [been to that house on the tape before]."

In elaborating on his relationship with R. Kelly in the years immediately leading up to the singer's arrest, namely 1998 through 2002, Carey Kelly painted a portrait of a distant relationship at best, which he characterized as one in which "I haven't really even been around, I really don't know what he do in his personal life, I can't actually answer that...To be realistic, I'm not in the man's personal life." In further fleshing out the allegations, Carey painted the family relationship as equally distant, such that, while Kelly "has helped us out in the past, you know, a lot of people go through things and have their own problems. You know, a lot of things they have to deal with themselves...I don't really talk to my sister much...I really don't know where she stay at...He's a busy man, he probably barely sees his kids, or probably take them on tour or whatever, so if he barely sees his kids, he ain't going to see mine, so that's just how it is. When you're in the lime light, and its busy like that, its hard." That Carey Kelly had such limited exposure to his brother in the years leading up to the sex tape surfacing serves as the most convincing evidence that he would have had no opportunity to utilize Kelly's homes in such a personal fashion, and moreover, would have had the type of close-knit relationship in which R. Kelly would have felt comfortable allowing his younger brother to utilize his homes in such an explicit manner.

Additionally, given the time frame in which the main tape was made, pegged between late 1998 and early 1999, a period in which both men were married, whomever appeared in the videos engaging in multiple sexual encounters was definitely guilty of adultery, if nothing else. In the case of Carey Kelly, he painted himself as a family man and devoted father with school-aged children in multiple interviews, countering the notion that he would have even been engaging in sex with women outside of his wife given the fact that he was happily married in the late 1990s. Moreover, according to Carey Kelly, the existence of the tape alone was causing his family unwanted turmoil and the allegations that Kelly's defense team seemed prepared to lodge were only making matters worse for his kids, to the point where "the family is just going through a lot of problems, I have kids that go to school, and you know, my kids, they brag on, 'You know, that's my uncle', and things of that nature, and other kids is like, 'I heard that's your daddy.' So there's a lot of emotional things going on [as a result of this tape], and that's crazy."

In addressing the bottom-line issue of whose face appeared on the tape, Carey Kelly, while denying any explicit knowledge of the tape's origin or of a larger problem on R. Kelly's part with underage women, Kelly's younger brother remained steadfast in his contention that it was not his face on the tape, "I have no idea who is supposed to be on the tape…[I just know] its not me, its not me in the videotape." Moreover, while Carey denied enough knowledge of his brother's personal life to offer any insight into whether R. Kelly had a fetish for underage girls consistent with the content of the tapes, he was willing to acknowledge that whoever appeared on the tape bared enough resemblance to R. Kelly for him to conclude they were one in the same person, "I can't actually say [what he's into] because I haven't been in that man's personal life, but that's his face [on the tape]."

In terms of Carey's ability to offer any informed opinion on Kelly's sexual preferences which might work to support or refute the charges lodged against the R&B star, his younger brother had nothing conclusive one way or the other, possibly in an effort to show support by displaying ignorance on the subject. However, he was willing to acknowledge the possibility that the charges lodged against Kelly held truth by reasoning that you can never really know anybody completely—even your own sibling, "People have lived with people for 20 years, and they up and killed their whole family. You can't actually know somebody, you can know of them. I don't put nothing past nobody."

Concerning his level of contact with Kelly throughout the Spring of 2002 in the midst of the R&B singer's defense team was attempting to lay the Rap on his younger brother, Carey had explained that, "I haven't talked to him...I haven't been able to get in touch with him." Ironically, at a September 20th, 2002 hearing, as prosecutors also turned over to the defense upward of 1000 pages of evidence, and Kelly formally surrendered his passport, his brother appeared for the first time publicly in support of his brother. In addressing how the embattled R&B singer was holding up under the pressure of facing a possible 15 years in prison, a close Kelly confidant and prominent Chicago record store owner, George Daniels, told journalists that, "He's been holding up pretty good...but you can imagine how a person feels when they go through that. They're under a microscope, and the whole world sees."

The court was paying Kelly equal intensity, limiting his travel to Chicago for the majority of the summer, until an August 8th hearing when he was given permission to travel to Miami for a gig. Kelly's next hearing concerning the situation happened on November 1, 2002, where, according to VH.1.com news, "Over objections from prosecutors, Judge Vincent Gaughan granted Kelly's request to leave the state for seven days beginning November 12, according to the Cook County 's state's attorney's office...Kelly [was] scheduled to perform at Powerhouse, a concert sponsored by WWPR-FM [Power 105] on November 14 at the Continental Airlines Arena in East Rutherford, New Jersey. The concert will also feature Ja Rule, Ashanti, Busta Rhymes, Fat Joe, Erick Sermon, Faith Evans, Doug E. Fresh and Sean Paul."

As Kelly's day of reckoning approached, his problems only appeared to worsen as additional tapes began to surface, oddly enough found in a motor home, including several in which Kelly, according to a feature in *Vibe Magazine*, is featured "receiving oral sex from a fair-skinned girl whose face is obscured by her long black mane. The tape then cuts to Kelly performing cunnilingus on yet another young woman who's perched on an office swivel chair. This one, a dark-skinned girl with back-grazing micro-mini braids, happily returns the favor. After endless [sexual relations], Kelly [who doesn't wear condoms in any of the tapes] and the paramour engage in intercourse. Kelly never has conventional sex with the third girl who appears on the tape, and her face is never shown. She just works her enormous posterior for the camera, moving left to right, up and down, writhing against the wall in supposed ecstasy. Ever the perfectionist, Kelly, who seems unhappy with the woman's choice in underwear, hands her a pair of white, boy-cut panties decorated with red frilly lace. After quickly slipping the preferred panties over her own, the girl gets back to grinding. The scene ends some 15 minutes later with Kelly pouring bottled water on her bare buttocks."

With the existence of the latest tapes, which fortunately for Kelly didn't appear to have any underage female participants, eliminating their relevance to his criminal case outside of demonstrating a pattern on the R&B singer's part of taping his seemingly unknowing sexual partners, Kelly was swamped with additional civil suits, including suits by several additional women, including one in which, according to an NME.com/MTV.com press update: "[on April 29, 2002] 20-year-old Patrice Jones launched the latest action in Chicago claiming…that after meeting Kelly in December 1998 when she was 16, that he initiated a nine-month sexual relationship with her.

According to the suit, Jones met Kelly at the Rock and Roll McDonald's in Chicago, a tourist trap in downtown's River North neighborhood, on the evening of her prom, whereupon Kelly asked for Jones' number and invited her to visit him at his recording studio…and Kelly first had sex at a Chicago recording studio in January 1999 when she was 16. The suit claims she and the star had sex an average of two to three times per week at the recording studio…on his tour bus…and various Chicago hotels from January to August 1999…Jones estimates that she had sex with Kelly between 20 and 30 times prior to her 17th birthday. 'During their relationship…Kelly promised to teach…Jones various vocations in the music industry including operation of musical equipment and the making of music videos,' the suit reads. 'Kelly took advantage of his occupation or status, position of authority, and plaintiff, Patrice Jones, had trust and confidence in him to cause her to develop a dependent relationship in him.' The suit also alleges she became pregnant by Kelly in June 1999 and in September he 'coerced' her into having an abortion…which he paid for and had his employees arrange at Family Planning Associates in September of that year… Jones' attorney, Susan Loggans, said that the complaint is going to be hard to beat, since she has medical records to back up Jones' accusations, witnesses to Jones' and Kelly's alleged ongoing relationship and phone records indicating that she had his private line."

Kelly attempted, in a rather fumbled effort, to dismiss the Jones lawsuit, denying that he even knew her, and telling MTV's John Norris that, "Whoever this girl is, she has two names. We're fighting that case and we're going to win that case because there are a lot of lies around it."

Another plaintiff was Tina Woods, of age but filmed without her knowledge or consent, who, according to *MTV News*: "Plaintiff Montina 'Tina' Woods—a dancer who's toured with Kelly collaborators the Isley Brothers…filed a suit last Friday [May 24] in the Cook County Circuit Court in Chicago accusing Kelly of setting up a hidden camera and secretly taping their sexual encounter. She's seeking $50,000 in damages…The encounter, which Woods said took place at his recording studio, Chicago Trax, is among others that have been copied onto a single tape and sold under the title R. Kelly Triple-X on the streets of major cities such as New York, Chicago, Atlanta, and Detroit, as well as on the Internet…Woods also accuses Kelly of negligence in that he failed to keep the tape from being copied and distributed…'[Woods] had a right to privacy to prevent her personal image from being recorded for the purpose of [Woods] personal gratification and possible dissemination to the public,' the suit reads. 'R. Kelly should have known that this was likely to cause severe emotional harm and economic harm to [Woods]…R. Kelly knew or had to have known such distribution would cause irreparable harm to further employment opportunities by the negligent release of an unauthorized videotape of (Woods),' since she was also in the entertainment industry. Adding to Woods' emotional distress claim, the suit says she's been in isolation 'to avoid recognition and embarrassment.'"

In an even more bizarre lawsuit filed in connection with the R. Kelly videotapes, which made Kelly look even more guilty, a Private Investigator sued him on July, 19, 2002 for $75,000, under circumstances the MTV News reported as: "Charles Freeman alleges in his suit, filed at Jackson County Circuit Court last week, that he was hired by Kelly via private detective Jack Palladino late last August. Freeman claims it was agreed he would be paid $100,000 plus up to $40,000 in expenses to recover the stolen videotape, described as a performance tape…According to a contract between the two parties, Freeman was given two days to recover and return the tape. Freeman was then to pass a 'lie-detector' test to prove he knew of no other copies 'whether in whole or in part in any form.' Freeman was also to keep all information about the tape confidential. He claims to have only been paid $65,000 for keeping his side of the bargain. Freeman's lawyer Gregory Vleisides, says he has not seen the tape and does not know why it is so valuable."

Some pundits, at the time, argued that this suit marked the most clear and convincing evidence yet of Kelly's guilt, rationalizing the suit made Kelly look as though his hiring of the detective to find the mysterious tape in 2001 was part of an attempt to diffuse the scandal before it could erupt by finding what could have been the principal sex tape before it could fall into the media's hands. Unfortunately, if that was the case, Kelly had failed, and in ignoring the P.I.'s bill, Kelly could have arguably been venting frustration at his failure to keep his illegal fetish under wraps.

In all, things were looking particularly bleak for Kelly by the fall of 2002 as he was battling charges on both the criminal and civil front. Amid the mounting civil claims against Kelly, his principal civil attorney, Gerald Margolis, attacked the onslaught of suits as frivolous, proclaiming that "enough is enough, perhaps…people have gotten the idea that R. Kelly is some sort of walking ATM machine they can hit up for cash simply by threatening to sue him. The cash machine is closed." Margolis additionally attempted to explain away Kelly's previous pattern of settling suits as not reflective of guilt on his client's part, but rather an effort to take "the high road with regard to a series of terrible allegations made against Robert. Rather than going to court to defend him against these charges, a process that would have degraded everyone concerned, we decided to settle the cases quietly. This latest suit is a collection of half-truths, distortions, and outright lies that we intend to fight and beat." Kelly's attorney also threw in for good measure that "R. Kelly is no angel, but he is no monster either."

Regardless of what Kelly's highly-paid representatives were saying in an effort to defend him, the singer was keeping a low profile, staying largely out-of-sight of the media, outside of required court appearances, and a handful of concert appearances, most of which had been scheduled prior to the child pornography charges being formally filed against him. With his future uncertain, Kelly, along with the watching world, could do little but sit captive, waiting out his fate like a death row inmate with the hours ticking down, praying on some mystery witness who would Pop out of thin air to exonerate him, giving Kelly amnesty from his own conscience and from what appeared at the time to be his probable guilt.

Epilogue

"Chocolate Factory"

On Wednesday, January 22, 2003, R. Kelly, already facing 21 felony counts of child pornography, was arrested a second time in six months on charges of a like nature, this time for possession of 12 photos of a nude girl discovered during a search of the singer's rented Davenport, Florida home at the time of his initial arrest. Taken into custody at the Grand Bay Hotel in Coconut Grove, Florida, Kelly was held based on police discovery of 12 digital images that depicted an underage female, three of which depicted Kelly involved in sexual conduct with the female minor. According to Chip Thullbery, spokesman for the Florida State Attorney's office, "even though the evidence was seized last summer, the pictures themselves did not establish a case…We had to confirm the identity of the girl, establish that the pictures were real, not computer-generated, and all of that takes time." Kelly had been in town for the video shoot of 'Ignition Remix', the first single off his new album. Interestingly, Kelly had a unique PR opportunity with the visual presentation of the shoot to work at altering his raunchy, erotic image, namely by toning it down dramatically, and according to an MTV account of the shoot, he did so without losing the upbeat tempo and energy he intended the remix to capture. Still, Kelly couldn't escape his trademark presence of female company, such that, according to MTV, "R. Kelly discovers a honey-filled haven in his new video for the 'Ignition Remix.' Shot two weeks ago in Miami, the video finds Kelly inviting an assortment of party goers into his black stretch Hummer. Once inside the vehicle, they find themselves in a hot spot called Club Jeep…'It's the remix to 'Ignition', hot and fresh out the kitchen,' Kelly sings, bouncing around in an assortment of basketball jerseys, including a special-ized top with the letters TLC on the front and Jam Master Jay's name on the back. He closes the video out by turning his back to the camera and paying homage to the late DJ."

Upon being detained, Kelly was transported to the Turner Guilford Knight Correctional Facility, where he was held for several hours before posting a $12,000 bond (at $1,000 per count). His publicity team immediately attempted to fan the rekindling flame that had calmed into a smolder of occasional headlines throughout the fall, and during a time in which Kelly was attempting to test the waters again with the release of a new album, 'Chocolate Factory', due in stores a month later, on February 18, with spokesman Alan Mayer arguing that "at this point…it looks to us like a classic case of piling on, in which a local jurisdiction tries to make headlines by attaching itself to a celebrity case. As far as we can tell, the charges all relate to R. Kelly's arrest last summer. In other words, there is nothing new here." Sadly, that fact, true or not for Kelly's legal case, couldn't have been more true in terms of its immediate reinforcement of the American public's larger impression of Kelly as someone who 'had a problem with underaged women,' whether he would ultimately be found criminally liable for that problem or not.

The latter impression became more explicit a month later. On Feb-ruary 18, 2003, when the press learned that Kelly was once again under investigation in Cook County for allegedly sexually assault-ing a 24-year-old woman in a Chicago Recording Studio. Accord-ing to MTV news, "police said they were investigating the complaint…but said no charges (had) been filed (yet.)" With little more information from which to dray any solid conclusions, the celebrity gossip-mill began again to fan the flames of controversy with their own speculation over the authenticity and larger relevance of the latest allegations. Kelly's publicists adhered to their usual line of defense, namely that the charges were frivolous, and more importantly, that there was little coincidence that "coming as they did on the same day R. Kelly is releasing what is likely to be the most successful album of his career...these supposed charges amount to nothing more than an outrageous and blatant attempt at character assassination. The fact is that R. Kelly did not assault anyone or engage in any improper behavior yesterday or any day, and he is confident that an impartial investigation will confirm that." Unfortunately, these investigations took time, and in the meanwhile, all Kelly was ultimately left to work with was a media partial to portraying him as continually embattled, whether they drew out any direct conclusions or not in the process of doing so. And the negative press surrounding Kelly's latest legal troubles, some positive commentary began to emerge from music critics on the quality of the music embodied in Kelly's latest album, 'Chocolate Factory.' Among the more glowing reviews, *USA Today* called the album "If anything, his current circumstances have fired his creative juices, and he digs deeper for some of his best work in years. Kelly, who wrote and produced all of the 100-plus minutes of music here, sings with emotional urgency over richly textured beats. He avoids unnecessary histrionics, and songs come off more like intense conversations. How that will translate into sales remains to be seen, but the singer's career seems to have rebounded from the initial battering...Kelly can let his music do the talking, and fans won't be disappointed when they sample what Chocolate Factory offers," while BET.com praised Kelly's latest effort as "undeniably one of the best records of his career....There are so few albums these days that stand together as a complete package. Chocolate Factory does that and more. It has the potential to be one of those classic records that you can clean the house to on Sunday afternoons and can make love to on Saturday night...It's as though his troubles outside the studio helped him to find a peaceful space inside it."

Finally, while it wasn't the last word on Kelly's legal or commercial fate, fans spoke up equally as loudly as critics in Kelly's favor via the stellar first week sales of Kelly's new album, scooping upward of 700,000 copies, and giving Kelly a debut in the top 5 of Billboard's Top 200 Album Chart. The latter chart performance indicates, if nothing else, that no one questions Kelly's musical genius, only his judgment with respect to the larger issue of using the celebrity that musical genius and its success afforded him to violate the trust of his fans, and more importantly, their very innocence.

All Kelly should truly hope for, in the end, is that he will have the forgiveness of the one man whom he has sought an audience with his entire career in spite of the millions of earthly fans Kelly already had listening—that he will one day perform in the halls of Heaven, before the eyes of God, robed in a redemption that he will never likely find in our naturally imperfect world. Keeping this in mind, Kelly's talent and life may end up tragically if his private life continues to become larger than his public one as a musical superstar. Still, despite how small his star may fade, he does shine bright and divine on millions of lives that otherwise would have had no one to inspire or remind them that at heart, we are all God's children. We should pray that one day Robert Kelly realizes that he has this power for the sake of his own soul.

Chart History

1992

January

▼ Kelly, as a member of Public Announcement, released Born Into The 90's. The LP went platinum and contained the hits "She's Got That Vibe," "Dedicated," "Honey Love," and "Slow Dance (Hey Mr. DJ)."

June

▼ Born Into The 90's was certified gold.

1993

January

▼ Born Into The 90's was certified platinum.

November

▼ By the end of the year, R. Kelly was on his own and he released 12 Play. Kelly's sexy lyrics took him the top of the pop charts with "Bump N' Grind" and found success with the tracks "Your Body's Callin'" and "Sex Me (Parts I & II)."

December

▼ The single "Sex Me (Parts I & II)" was certified gold.

1994

January

▼ 12 Play was certified platinum.

February

▼ Kelly hit the Top 40 with "Bump N' Grind."

March

▼ 12 Play and the single "Bump N' Grind" were certified platinum.

▼ Kelly hit the Top 10 with "Bump N' Grind."

April

▼ Kelly hit #1 for a week with "Bump N' Grind."

May

▼ Kelly hit the Top 40 with "Your Body's Callin'."

▼ While Kelly continued to reap the rewards of a his hit LP throughout the year, he also produced the debut LP by Aaliyah. By the end of the summer, rumors of a marriage between Kelly and the 15-year old songstress had surfaced.

June
- ▼ 12 Play was certified 3x platinum.

July
- ▼ The single "Your Body's Callin'" was certified gold.

1995

January
- ▼ Kelly was nominated for an American Music Award for Favorite Soul/R&B Album.
- ▼ Kelly found himself on the top of pop and R&B charts again, but this time as songwriter and co-producer for Michael Jackson's "You Are Not Alone."
- ▼ Kelly appeared on the soundtrack for Low Down Dirty Shame with a remix of "Homie, Lover, Friend."

September
- ▼ 12 Play was certified 4x platinum.

November
- ▼ Kelly released R. Kelly. The LP reflected a change for Kelly with less emphasis on suggestive and sexual lyrics, and help from gospel singer, Kirk Franklin, and rapper, The Notorious B.I.G.
- ▼ Kelly topped the Billboard R&B Singles chart for a week and the Singles Sales chart for a week with "You Remind Me Of Something."
- ▼ Kelly hit the Top 40 with "You Remind Me Of Something."

December
- ▼ R. Kelly topped the Billboard Pop Albums chart for a week and the R&B Albums chart for 2 weeks.
- ▼ Kelly hit the Top 10 with "You Remind Me Of Something."

1996

January
- ▼ R. Kelly was certified 2x platinum and the single "You Remind Me Of Something" was certified platinum.

February
- ▼ R. Kelly was nominated for a Grammy Award for Song of the Year (songwriting nomination for Michael Jackson's "You Are Not Alone."

March
- ▼ Kelly hit the Top 40 with "Down Low (Nobody Has To Know)."
- ▼ Kelly topped the Billboard Hot R&B Singles chart for 7 weeks, the Hot R&B Singles Sales chart for 7 weeks, the Hot R&B Singles Airplay chart for a week, and the Dance Music Maxi-Singles Sales chart for 3 weeks with "Down Low (Nobody Has To Know)."

April
▼ The single "Down Low (Nobody Has To Know)" was certified platinum and hit the Top 10.

June
▼ 12 Play was certified 5x platinum and R. Kelly was certified 3x platinum.

▼ Kelly hit the Top 40 with "I Can't Sleep Baby (If I)."

August
▼ Kelly topped the Billboard Hot R&B Singles chart for 2 weeks with "I Can't Sleep Baby (If I)."

▼ Kelly hit the Top 10 with "I Can't Sleep Baby (If I)."

September
▼ The single "I Can't Sleep (If I)" was certified platinum.

▼ The video for "Down Low (Nobody Has To Know)" was nominated for an MTV Video Music Award for Best Male Video.

November
▼ Kelly hit the Top 40 with "I Believe I Can Fly" from the Space Jams soundtrack.

December
▼ "I Believe I Can Fly" topped the Billboard Hot 100 Singles Sales chart for 7 weeks, the Hot R&B Singles chart for 6 weeks, the Hot R&B Singles Sales chart for 5 weeks, and the Hot R&B Singles Airplay chart for 2 weeks.

▼ Kelly hit the Top 10 with "I Believe I Can Fly."

1997

January
▼ Kelly began the year at a Kirk Franklin concert announcing that his musical direction was now directed at the Lord instead of the libido.

▼ Kelly was nominated for an American Music Award for Favorite Soul/R&B Male Artist.

▼ "I Believe I Can Fly" topped the Billboard R&B Singles Sales chart for 5 weeks.

▼ The single "I Believe I Can Fly" was certified platinum.

April
▼ Kelly topped the UK Singles chart with "I Believe I Can Fly" for 3 weeks.

June
▼ Kelly hit the Top 40 with "Gotham City" from the Batman And Robin soundtrack.

August
▼ Kelly hit the Top 10 with "Gotham City."

September
- ▼ The single "Gotham City" was certified gold.
- ▼ Kelly was nominated for 2 MTV Video Music Awards including Best Male Video and Best Video from a Film ("I Believe I Can Fly").

October
- ▼ R. Kelly was certified 4x platinum.

1998

February
- ▼ R. Kelly took home 3 Grammy Awards for Best R&B Song, Best Song Written Specifically for a Motion Picture, and Best Male R&B Vocal Performance ("I Believe I Can Fly") and was also nominated for Record Of The Year and Song of the Year ("I Believe I Can Fly").

March
- ▼ R. Kelly won a BMI Award for Pop Songwriter of the Year ("I Believe I Can Fly," "I Can't Sleep Baby (If I)," and "I Don't Want To" (recorded by Toni Braxton)).

April
- ▼ Kelly was arrested in Chicago for disorderly conduct for a loud car stereo. Kelly reportedly refused to turn down his stereo and got verbally abusive.

May
- ▼ 2 of the 3 charges were dropped (including disorderly conduct), but Kelly was still charged with a noise violation.
- ▼ Kelly hit the Top 40 helping out Sparkle with "Be Careful" from her LP Sparkle.
- ▼ "Be Careful" topped the Billboard R&B Singles Airplay chart for 6 weeks.

July
- ▼ The noise violation charges were dropped with no explanation given.
- ▼ Kelly appeared on the soundtrack for Wood with "It's All Good."

November
- ▼ Kelly released the double set, R. with the first single "I'm Your Angel" —a duet with Celine Dion—hitting the Top 40.
- ▼ R. topped the Billboard R&B Albums chart for a week.

December
- ▼ R. was certified 3x platinum and the single "I'm Your Angel" was certified platinum and hit the Top 10.
- ▼ "I'm Your Angel" topped the Billboard Hot 100 Singles chart, the Hot 100 Singles Sales chart for 6 weeks, and the Adult Contemporary chart for 12 weeks.

1999

January
- ▼ R. was certified 4x platinum.
- ▼ Kelly hit#1 with "I'm Your Angel" (with Celine Dion) and the Top 40 with "When A Woman's Fed Up"

February
- ▼ At the Grammy Awards, R. Kelly was nominated for Best Pop Collaboration with Vocals ("I'm Your Angel" (with Celine Dion)) and Best R&B Performance by a Duo or Group with Vocal ("Lean On Me" (with Kirk Franklin, Mary J. Blige, Bono, & Crystal Lewis)).

June
- ▼ R. Kelly was certified 5x platinum.
- ▼ R. Kelly won 2 Soul Train Music Awards for Best R&B/Soul Album, Male (R.) and the Sammy Davis Jr. Entertainer of the Year Award. Kelly was also nominated for Best R&B/Soul Single, Male ("Half On A Baby").

August
- ▼ R. Kelly was named R&B Artist of the Year at the Source Hip-Hip Music Awards.
- ▼ R. was certified 5x platinum.

September
- ▼ R. Kelly hit the Top 40 as featured on Puff Daddy's "Satisfy You" and with his own hit, "If I Could Turn Back The Hands Of Time."

October
- ▼ "Satisfy You" topped the Billboard Hot 100 Singles Sales chart for 3 weeks, the Billboard R&B/Hip-Hop Singles & Tracks chart for 2 weeks, and the Billboard Rap Singles chart for 4 weeks.

December
- ▼ R. Kelly won a Billboard Music Award for R&B/Hip-Hop Artist of the Year.

2000

January
- ▼ Kelly won an American Music Award for Favorite Male Soul/R&B Artist.
- ▼ Kelly returned to the Top 40 featured on Puff Daddy's "Satisfy You."

February
- ▼ Kelly was nominated for a few Grammy Awards including Best Male R&B Vocal Performance ("When A Woman's Fed Up"), Best R&B Album (R.) and Best Rap Performance by a Duo or Group ("Satisfy You" with Puff Daddy).

March
 ▼ R. Kelly won a Soul Train Music Award for Best R&B/Soul or Rap Album (R.).

May
 ▼ R. was certified 6x platinum.

June
 ▼ R. Kelly could be heard on the soundtrack for Shaft with "Bad Man" and the soundtrack for Nutty Professor 2: The Klumps with "Just A Touch."

November
 ▼ R. Kelly's next LP, TP-2.com was released.
 ▼ TP-2.com hit #1 on the Billboard 200 LP Chart and the Billboard R&B / Hip-Hop Chart for 3 weeks.
 ▼ R. Kelly hit #1 for 2 weeks on the Billboard R&B/Hip Hot chart with "I Wish" and hit the Top 40 (re-entering in February).
 ▼ R. Kelly was certified 7x platinum.

December
 ▼ TP-2.com was certified 2x platinum.

2001

February
 ▼ Kelly was nominated for a Grammy Award for Best Male R&B Vocal Performance ("I Wish").

March
 ▼ TP-2.com was certified 3x platinum.
 ▼ Kelly won 2 Soul Train Music Awards for Best R&B/Soul Single, Male ("I Wish") and Best R&B/Soul Album, Male (TP-2.com) and was nominated for Best R&B/Soul or Rap Album.
 ▼ Kelly won 2 NAACP Image Award for Outstanding Male Artist and Outstanding Music Video ("I Wish").

April
 ▼ Kelly was nominated for a Blockbuster Entertainment Award for Favorite Male Artist —R&B.

May
 ▼ Kelly hit the Top 40 with "Fiesta" (with Jay-Z).

June
 ▼ Kelly hit #1 on the Billboard R&B/Hip-Hop Singles & Tracks chart for 5 weeks and the R&B/Hip-Hop Airplay chart for a week with "Fiesta" (with Jay-Z).
 ▼ Kelly could be heard on the soundtrack for Fast And The Furious with "Take My Time Tonight."

September
- ▼ Kelly's video for "I Wish" was nominated for a MTV Video Music Award for Best R&B Video.
- ▼ Kelly won a Source Award for R&B Artist of the Year.

October
- ▼ The single "If I Could Turn Back The Hands Of Time" was certified gold.
- ▼ Kelly hit the Top 40 with "Feelin' On Yo Booty."

November
- ▼ Kelly could be heard on the soundtrack for Ali with "The World's Greatest" and "Hold On."

December
- ▼ Kelly hit the Top 40 with "The World's Greatest."
- ▼ Kelly topped Billboard Year-End Charts as Top R&B/ Hip-Hop Artist, Top R&B/Hip-Hop Album (TP-2.com), Top Hot R&B/Hip-Hop Singles & Tracks ("Fiesta"), Top R&B/Hip-Hop Artist —Male, Top R&B/Hip-Hop Album Artist, and Top R&B/Hip-Hop Album Artist - Male.

2002

January
- ▼ Kelly was nominated for 2 American Music Awards for Favorite Male Pop/Rock Artist and Favorite Male Soul/R&B Artist.

February
- ▼ Kelly hit the Top 40 helping out Fat Joe with "We Thuggin'" and hit the Top 10 with "The World's Greatest."
- ▼ Kelly performed at the opening ceremonies of the Winter Olympics in Utah.
- ▼ Controversy hit Kelly when a newspaper in Chicago said they anonymously received video footage showing Kelly have sex with an underage girl.
- ▼ Kelly teamed up with Jay-Z for the LP The Best of Both Worlds.

April
- ▼ The Best Of Both Worlds topped the Billboard Hot R&B/Hip-Hop Album chart.
- ▼ TP-2.com was certified 4x platinum.
- ▼ Kelly's controversies surrounding the 'sex scandal' continued with Kelly settling 2 lawsuits against him made by families claiming the singer had sex with underage girls. Promotional appearances for The Best of Both Worlds were also cancelled. The allegations continued with former protégé, Sparkle, telling a radio station that one video tape Kelly is accused of being a part of also includes her then 14-year-old niece.

May
- ▼ The Best of Both Worlds was certified platinum.

▼ Another lawsuit was filed against Kelly—this time for invasion of privacy. The woman claims she was video taped without her consent on one of the alleged 'Kelly sex tapes.'

June

▼ Kelly was arrested on charges of producing child pornography—charges that were based on video tapes allegedly made by Kelly and allegedly showing Kelly engaged in sex with an under-aged girl.

November

▼ Kelly topped the R&B/Hip-Hop Singles Sales chart for 17 weeks with "Ignition."

▼ Kelly had several R&B hits with Jay-Z on the tracks "Get This Money," "The Best Of Both Worlds (Intro)," "Take You Home With Me a.k.a. Body," "Somebody's Girl," and "Shake Ya Body" (also with Lil' Kim), and the solo tracks "Heaven I Need A Hug" and "Step In The Name Of Love."

2003

▼ Singles Artist of the Year

January

▼ Kelly was arrested again for child pornography charges— this time in Florida—due to the finding of pictures of a sexual nature found in his home last year. Kelly was charged with 12 counts of child pornography possession.

February

▼ R. Kelly was nominated for a Soul Train Music Award with Jay-Z for R&B/Soul Album Group, Band or Duo (The Best Of Both Worlds).

▼ Kelly released his next LP, Chocolate Factory.

▼ Kelly was nominated for a Grammy Award for Best Male R&B Vocal Performance for ("The World's Greatest").

March

▼ Chocolate Factory sold over 532,000 copies in its first week of release and topped the charts.

▼ Kelly hit the Top 40 with "Ignition."

April

▼ Kelly recorded and released the single "Soldier's Heart"—a tribute the US military fighting in the war in Iraq. Kelly said of the single in a statement: "This song is my way of saying thank you to everyone protecting us and allowing us to sleep comfortable at night and send our children off to school in the morning." Proceeds of the single will go to the soldier's family.

▼ Kelly hit the Top 10 with "Ignition."

May

▼ Kelly topped the Billboard Top 40 Tracks chart and the UK Singles chart with "Ignition."

▼ Chocolate Factory was certified 2x platinum.

▼ Kelly could be heard on the soundtrack for 2 Fast 2 Furious with "Pick Up The Phone" (with Ludacris and Tyrese).

June

▼ Kelly topped the Billboard R&B/Hip-Hop Singles Sales chart with "Snake."

▼ Kelly won a BET Award for Best Male R&B Artist.

July

▼ Kelly hit the Top 40 with the help of Big Tigger with "Snake."

▼ Kelly began filming Eye Contact.

August

▼ Kelly's video for "Ignition" was nominated for a MTV Video Music Award for Best R&B Video.

▼ R. was certified 8x platinum.

September

▼ Kelly released a hits collection—The "R" In R&B Collection Volume 1.

November

▼ Kelly was nominated for 2 American Music Awards for Favorite Soul/R&B Male Artist and Favorite Soul/R&B Album.

▼ Kelly was honored at the Vibe Awards with the R&B Vanguard Award.

▼ Kelly could be heard on Missy Elliott's LP This Is Not A Test on the track "Dats What I'm Talkin About."

▼ The "R" In R&B Collection Volume 1 was certified platinum.

December

▼ Kelly topped the Billboard Hot R&B/Hip-Hop Singles & Tracks chart and Hot R&B/Hip-Hop Airplay chart with "Step in the Name of Love."

▼ Kelly had the 7th biggest selling LP of the year—Chocolate Factory—which sold over 2.4 million copies during the year in the US.

2004

February

▼ Kelly was nominated for 2 Grammy Awards including Best Contemporary R&B Album (Chocolate Factory) and Best Male R&B Vocal Performance ("Step in the Name Of Love").

▼ Kelly hit the Top 40 helping out Cassidy with "Hotel."

March

▼ Kelly won a Soul Train Music Award for R&B/Soul Album, Male (Chocolate Factory).

About the Author

Author Jake Brown works full-time in the recording industry as president of Nashville-based Versailles Records. Published and forthcoming titles include: *SUGE KNIGHT—The Rise, Fall & Rise of Death Row Records (A Hard-Hitting Study of One Man, One Company that Changed the Course of American Music Forever); YOUR BODY"S CALLING ME: The Life and Times of Robert R. Kelly (Music, Love, Sex, and Money)—An Unauthorized Biography*; and *READY TO DIE: THE STORY OF BIGGIE SMALLS— NOTORIOUS B.I.G.: King of the World & New York City (Fast Money, Puff Daddy, Faith, and Life After Death)—The Unauthorized Biography of Notorious B.I.G.*

ORDER FORM

WWW.AMBERBOOKS.COM
African-American Self Help and Career Books

Fax Orders: 480-283-0991   Postal Orders: Send Checks & Money Orders to:
Telephone Orders: 480-460-1660   Amber Books Publishing
Online Orders: E-mail: Amberbks@aol.com   1334 E. Chandler Blvd., Suite 5-D67
Phoenix, AZ 85048

_____ *Your Body's Calling Me: The Life & Times of "Robert" R. Kelly*
_____ *The House that Jack Built*
_____ *Langhorn & Mary: A 19th American Century Love Story*
_____ *The African-American Woman's Guide to Great Sex, Happiness, & Marital Bliss*
_____ *The Afrocentric Bride: A Style Guide*
_____ *Beautiful Black Hair: A Step-by-Step Instructional Guide*
_____ *How to Get Rich When You Ain't Got Nothing*
_____ *The African-American Job Seeker's Guide to Successful Employment*
_____ *The African-American Travel Guide*
_____ *Suge Knight: The Rise, Fall, and Rise of Death Row Records*
_____ *The African-American Teenagers Guide to Personal Growth, Health, Safety, Sex and Survival*
_____ *Get That Cutie in Commercials, Televisions, Films & Videos*
_____ *Wake Up and Smell the Dollars! Whose Inner City is This Anyway?*
_____ *How to Own and Operate Your Home Day Care Business Successfully Without Going Nuts!*
_____ *The African-American Woman's Guide to Successful Make-up and Skin Care*
_____ *How to Play the Sports Recruiting Game and Get an Athletic Scholarship:*
_____ *Is Modeling for You? The Handbook and Guide for the Young Aspiring Black Model*

Name:_____

Company Name:_____

Address:_____

City:_____State:_____Zip:_____

Telephone: (_____) _____E-mail:_____

Your Body's Calling Me	$12.95	❏ Check ❏ Money Order ❏ Cashiers Check
The House That Jack Built	$16.95	❏ Credit Card: ❏ MC ❏ Visa ❏ Amex ❏ Discover
Langhorn & Mary	$25.95	
Great Sex	$14.95	CC#_____
The Afrocentric Bride	$16.95	
Beautiful Black Hair	$16.95	Expiration Date:_____
How to Get Rich	$14.95	**Payable to:**
Job Seeker's Guide	$14.95	Amber Books
Travel Guide	$14.95	1334 E. Chandler Blvd., Suite 5-D67, Phoenix, AZ 85048
Suge Knight	$21.95	
Teenagers Guide	$19.95	**Shipping:** $5.00 per book. Allow 7 days for delivery.
Cutie in Commercials	$16.95	**Sales Tax:** Add 7.05% to books shipped to Arizona addresses.
Wake Up & Smell the Dollars	$18.95	
Home Day Care	$12.95	**Total enclosed: $**_____
Successful Make-up	$14.95	
Sports Recruiting:	$12.95	For Bulk Rates Call: **480-460-1660**
Modeling:	$14.95	**ORDER NOW**